A CASE FOR EXCELLENCE

CASE STUDIES IN CONGREGATIONAL MINISTRY

Compiled by

GLENN L. BORRESON

CSS Publishing Company, Inc., Lima, Ohio

A CASE FOR EXCELLENCE

Library of Congress Cataloging-in-Publication Data

Borreson, Glenn L., 1944-
    A case for excellence : Case studies in congregational ministry / Glenn L. Borreson.
        p.   cm.
    ISBN 0-7880-1182-0 (pbk.)
    1. Pastoral theology—Case studies.   I. Title.
BV4011.B59   1998
263'.07'22—dc21   97-26638
                                                                                CIP

ISBN 0-7880-1182-0

To
my colleagues in ministry
who are, with me,
both teachers and learners

Table Of Contents

PART TWO

Counseling And Relationships

Foreword

There have been several significant "break" points in my career, when I "moved up a level" in my practice of ministry — learning to steal sermons, seminary, Clinical Pastoral Education, doctorate, time in the Holy Land, learning *not* to steal sermons, cancer, The Academy of Parish Clergy (APC). All of those experiences added immeasurably to my own Christian growth, but the one I'd hold onto the longest *for the sake of my own ministry* is APC. That's for many reasons, but the case study method is high among them.

I started as a parish pastor but was "sidetracked" into a decade in campus ministry and a doctoral program. Then I returned to the parish. How things had changed in those ten years — civil rights, Vietnam, women's liberation, lay empowerment! The church I had pastored no longer existed. I needed help in becoming a pastor in the new church.

Such help was surprisingly difficult to come by. It's hard to remember now, when continuing education for ministers is a big business not only for seminaries and denominations, but for travel agents, colleges, consultants, think tanks, hospitals, and zoos, but CPE was about the only continuing education around in those days. D.Min. programs were in their infancy. Ministers were expected to go to seminary and have good memories of what they learned there, which usually had more to do with what happened to the Amorites than how to deal with the mother of the bride or a grieving widower.

Individually, when ministers got together in judicatory meetings to listen to out-of-state preachers and announcements of coming events, they participated in the "complain and brag" syndrome, and were quite willing to offer theoretical "advice" to others, especially new pastors. Ministers worked alone, however, and were not used to actual observation of their peers at work, or being observed by them. Also, they received a great deal of unsolicited criticism by church members, criticism meant more to ventilate the members than to educate the ministers, so they tended to be afraid of "evaluation" and thus not very open to sharing their practice.

I needed these people, though. I knew the folks who actually practiced it were the real experts in parish ministry. How could I get into their practices, to learn from them? Then I heard about a new professional group for parish ministers. Its very motto was "Excellence in Ministry Through Sharing the Practice." Its members wanted to learn from one another and were working on facilitating that learning. I joined APC and became a part of a case study group. It not only smoothed my transition back into parish work, it changed my ministry.

The thrust of APC case studies wasn't just to learn from our peers, as valuable as that was, but to learn how to observe our own practice and to learn from our own work, in our own parishes, all the time. We learned how to observe, evaluate, plan, and be proactive, not just reactive. We learned how to learn — not just from written documents or theories of others, but from our own experiences.

Best of all, it was ecumenical. Baptists and Presbyterians and Roman Catholics and Lutherans and all the others of my new friends had a different angle of vision on ministry, from me and from one another. We were giving one another ideas we would never have come up with on our own, or in groups of our own denominational peers. Soon, whenever any issue or need arose in my ministry, I found myself listening for the voices of my case study colleagues. What would Father Mike say about this? Baptist Bob? Sister Mary Jane? I loved reading the cases Glenn Borreson has compiled here; I got to hear the voices of my friends again.

I'm grateful to James Glasse and C. David Jones and APC and all the others who have brought the case study method to ministry. We are better for it. Case studies do not constitute some magic bullet that solves the problems of ministry, but they do provide us with order and vision, with a way of learning in all that we do, with better possibilities of service to God and our congregations.

John Robert McFarland
United Methodist Church
Charleston, Illinois

Introduction

One of the untapped resources for growth among clergy is other clergy. We readily go off to seminars, workshops, and classes in places near and far to learn from experts, and these opportunities are often helpful. We sometimes forget, however, that we who are colleagues on the front lines of everyday ministry do have knowledge, wisdom, and support which can be shared with one another. In some ways, we are the experts. This book is about one way to lay claim to being valuable resources to one another.

Case studies have been around for many years, and clergy in such groups as the Academy of Parish Clergy have been deliberately using them for more than twenty years as tools to encourage growth and excellence in the practice of ministry. Far too often in both our formal and informal clergy gatherings, our conversations have been, as one of us has succinctly said, either "complain or brag." The problem with that is that neither mode is really helpful, and instead of encouraging clergy to learn from one another, both modes are more likely to erect the human barrier of defensiveness or rouse the unruly demons of jealousy and despair. What we clergy need are ways to support and ways to learn from one another. We need each other in order to do better ministry.

The case study is a disciplined way of bringing clergy together to examine a slice from ministry and to learn from it and each other. Not only do clergy benefit from the individual gifts of each pastor present when the case is presented, but the method itself is directly related to ministry. It is specific and practical and, at the same time, can be the focus for the use of several disciplines. For example, in the same case theological, spiritual, administrative, pastoral care, and group dynamics issues all may impinge on the specific situation. The case study is a good tool to integrate learning for the sake of better ministry. Indeed, one goal might well be the presentation of ministry practice as "a case for excellence" or growth in faithful and effective ministry.

This book has two parts. The first presents a descriptive method for doing ministry case studies and follows it with more than thirty cases employing this method. The second part offers a consultation method, and this, too, is followed by additional case studies. The reader should note here at the beginning that the two methods bear marked similarities, but yet are quite distinct from each other and ought not be confused.

Case Study Methods

More than twenty years ago James Glasse began using the case study method successfully in his supervision of seminary students. His students would write up in a disciplined format a specific event from their recent ministry experience, and that past event — a case — would be reflected upon by other students under Glasse's guidance. This focused reflection on a past event would lead to learning about what went well, what did not, what contributed to effective ministry, and so on, with the insights of colleagues contributing to the learning.

Glasse's account of his discovery of this methodology is the first chapter in this book. He succeeded in giving a generation of clergy a new and effective tool for reflecting on ministry situations. This tool was not abstract, about what might take place some time in some place, but it was concrete, about what actually happened in this place to these people at this time. As time went on, however, not only was this methodology found useful in seminary situations, but clergy groups in many places adopted, and sometimes adapted, his case study method for themselves. Many of the cases in this book are from clergy who did exactly this.

As time has moved on, however, and the case study contributed to clergy learning, it was discovered that another methodology could be helpful to pastors. Glasse's method was very effective in examining past ministry events, but that time frame was also its limitation. Often the critical events of ministry are those which clergy are right in the middle of, and it would be helpful to reflect on them with colleagues in these immediate circumstances and not wait weeks or months until the event is past. Perhaps colleagues might even have a role in the outcome of such events if reflection could be engaged *in medias res*, in the middle of things.

C. David Jones' chapter which begins part two in this book makes such a case. From the viewpoint of a practicing pastor, he describes the limitations of Glasse's descriptive case study method and advocates what he calls "a clinical approach," or what I have called a consultation case study method. He builds on the methodology of Glasse but takes it a new turn by calling for case studies to be current, unfinished, if you will, cases in ministry. Colleagues become not just helpful critics of a past event which can no longer be changed, but they can become creative partners in considering how best to do ministry right now. The focus for this methodology is not the past, and perhaps indirectly the future, but the present and the future which may be quite directly affected by consultation with colleagues.

Argument can be made for either of these methods. Jones, in fact, strongly argues that his clinical, or I would say, consultation, case study offers clergy a better tool. I tend to agree with him. In fact, in the descriptive cases I have seen clergy present through the years, I have observed what I would call an almost intrinsic movement within many of them toward consultation, that is, to invite colleague responses to and advice in the unfinished aspects of their ministry situation. A critical element in both methods, I would insist, continues to be focusing on the case at hand and refusing to flee to advice giving, flights of fancy, or ministry comparisons. My basic purpose in including both case study methods is not to pose one against the other, but to present pastors with two distinct and yet related methods for effective reflection on ministry. A group of clergy could adopt either method and profit from using it. In fact, the methods are included in detail with the hope that these chapters, plus the actual cases which follow, will encourage more pastors to employ the case study for their mutual growth in ministry.

The Case Studies

The heart of this book is more than fifty cases from ministry in and with congregations. Before they came to be included in these pages, these cases were presented by pastors to small groups of colleagues. They usually describe an event, always a slice of ministry, from the practice of ordinary ministry. Whether a case

13

bears great evidence of the high calling or mostly scrapes and bruises from work in life's trenches, every case is one in which pastors have sought to be faithful practitioners.

Nearly all the cases follow Glasse's recommended typed single-space, one page length. Originally, the typed lines of the cases were numbered down the left edge of the paper for ease of reference within the group setting. This is omitted here. In addition, most of the cases originally had headings for the four or five sections clearly delineated by Glasse and Jones in their respective chapters. These likewise have been omitted, but the progression within cases is nearly always the same: from background to description to analysis to evaluation. The focus questions at the end of each case are my additions intended to increase the value to readers in their reflections, be these alone or within a small group.

Pastors from six denominations in nine states, many of them colleagues in the Academy of Parish Clergy, have graciously agreed to share cases from their ministry. I have sought to take great care in guarding the confidentiality of these colleagues, their congregations, and the people involved. General demographic information and denominational labels have been added, but virtually all names of local places and people plus occasional other details have been changed.

˙Why read these cases? To study ministry where all the disciplines come together — in the local congregation and community. These cases can be used for reflection alone or in small groups, by ministry students as well as pastors, by supervisors and interns. While many of these cases exemplify very good ministry, they are not presented because they represent an ideal, but because they illustrate their clergy/authors' efforts to grow in effectiveness.

Again, why read these cases? To be motivated to gather a group of clergy colleagues and do your own cases. These cases, the reader should note, are only half the story. The rest of the story is clergy gathered to read and discuss cases they themselves have written from their own ministry. My hope is for this to happen in many more places — to have pastors doing their own "case for excellence" and growth in their ministry.

Glenn L. Borreson

14

PART I

The Descriptive Case Study Method
by James D. Glasse*

This chapter is a description of the particular case method I have developed. By doing this I do not mean to imply that this is the best form of the case method, nor that the case method is the only one. This is simply what I know best. And, in the manner of the case method, I will take time to tell the story of how I stumbled into it, how it has developed, and what I have learned through the use of it with both seminary students and parish clergy. What follows is designed to enable groups of pastors to begin to use the case method.

A. I Discover The Case Method

My own use of the case method grew out of my need to find a way to supervise the field education of students at Vanderbilt Divinity School. I did not have the time, the energy, or the training to do much personal supervision "in the field." I needed to find a way to work with students at my convenience on campus. I began organizing "field education seminars." The seminars met for one hour each week and consisted of small groups of students who were at work in a variety of field settings. The students seemed to enjoy and profit from these informal opportunities for discussion each week. I found them invaluable as a way of keeping in touch with what students were facing in the field and how they were relating these experiences to their studies in the seminary.

But very early I became aware that the sessions were not uniformly helpful, either to me or to the students. Some days we would spend an hour listening to the students tell about a problem they faced in the parish. At the end of the hour the teller felt better for having "talked it out" with peers, and the others felt that they had been "helpful." But the hour was over before the issues were

---

*This chapter, originally titled "A Case Method for Pastors," is from *Putting It Together in the Parish*, by James D. Glasse. Copyright © 1972 by Abingdon Press. Slightly altered by permission of Abingdon Press.

focused for the group, and there was little opportunity for careful analysis or serious evaluation. I began the search for a style of seminar which would be open on one end to the emerging experiences of students in the field, and open on the other end to their structured life of learning in the seminary. What I needed was a device to focus the work of the seminar on concrete cases, although at the time I did not know how to develop such a device.

B. The Idea Of The "Event"

It appeared to me that the basic problem in getting at issues lay in the fact that discussions in the seminars tended to alternate between anecdotes on the one hand (detailed, concrete, personal reports that were not really open to the perception of the group) and abstractions on the other hand (general ideas about ministry, programs, doctrines). What was needed, therefore, was a way to present concrete instances of practice to a group of peers for purposes of learning. The possibility of a "case study" of an "event" commended itself. I used the term "event" because it was a neutral term, making it clear that I wanted descriptions not of "problems" or "issues" or "failures" or "successes," but of a piece of practice which could be presented to the seminar for analysis and evaluation.

Events are, by definition, occasions in which the professionals act as responsible agents. These are not happenings they observe, but events in which they participate. Reports of these events, then, will reveal the character of their involvement, their commitment, and their competence. By requiring students to write cases out of their own involvement, I meant to suggest that they were, themselves, involved in situations of some importance and that they could learn from reflection on their own activities.

C. Writing The Case

Because of the limitations under which I began to work (a small group of relatively inexperienced students who met only one hour each week to discuss their field experience), I developed a form of case writing and a discipline for discussing them under those limitations. I have continued to use the same form with groups of

18

parish clergy. Here is the memorandum I prepared to describe the discipline of case-writing. It is sent to pastors, along with sample cases, to guide their preparation for a "case conference."

Memorandum to Ministers:

The case conference is based on case material provided by the ministers who participate. I set the structure. You provide the content. The structure provides a method for getting hold of issues in practice. The cases provide both the content and context of the issues. We do not discuss "subjects" or "issues" or "problems" in the abstract. We deal with cases — accounts of events in ministerial practice. When we meet for the case conference we will "get down to cases." But first we must have the cases.

1. The case must be written: A "case" is a written report of an event in which you were involved as a minister with some responsibility for the outcome. The purpose of writing the case is to produce a record of the event.

2. The written case must be brief: The case report is to be written on one side of a single sheet of paper — no longer. Part of the discipline is to learn what can be condensed into this limited space. Limitations of space force the writer to identify critical information.

3. The case must have four parts: The four parts are to be clearly distinguished. They need not be equal in length. But each of the parts must be included, or the case cannot be discussed at the conference.

(a) Background: enough information to set the event in context. What you had in mind, what you hoped/feared would happen, when and how you became aware of/involved in the event, what pressure and persons precipitated and shaped the event.

(b) Description: what happened and what you did. Report the event, including as much detail as possible in the limited space.

(c) Analysis: identify issues and relationships, with special attention to changes and resistance to change. Try to answer the question: What's going on here?

(d) Evaluation: your estimate of your own effectiveness in the event. Did you do what you set out to do? Did you function effectively? If so, why? If not, why not? What factors or forces emerged which you did not anticipate? What questions might the group discuss that would be most helpful to you?

4. Clarify the question of confidentiality: If you do not want to reveal the identity of persons and institutions, use fictitious names and addresses (Mrs. A, Mr. B, X Church, Y town). If you reveal identity, but wish the information to be confidential in the group, write at the top: "CONFIDENTIAL: For conference use only."

D. The Case Conference

Cases become the subject matter for tightly structured seminar sessions in which (a) a group of ministers or seminary students (b) assume clearly defined roles (c) for the discussion of a specific case according to a strict docket. The design of the case conference, like the form of the written case, grew out of the limitations under which I began to develop my own case method. I continue to use it with various kinds of groups, partly because I am familiar with it, and partly to test one very limited method under a variety of conditions.

(a) The group may vary in size from three to twelve persons. I prefer a group of six to ten because of the strict limits of time under which I choose to work. My objectives in using a group are: to help them discover the resources for professional self-education that exist in the group, to help them learn that they can learn from one another, and to help them grow in their ability to trust their

20

colleagues to assist them in improving their professional competence. Members of the group may vary widely in age, experience, and ability. It does not seem to matter much whether they are similar in denomination, training, or professional status. In fact, one of the discoveries in every group is the "variety of gifts" in the group.

(b) Three clearly distinguished roles are played by members of the group.

The "presenter" has written the case and has distributed it to members of the group in advance of the seminar.

The "discussants" have received their copies in advance and are required to spend at least one hour in studying the case.

The "leader" has consulted with the presenter, helped to write the case, and is responsible for the conduct of the case conference.

(c) The case conference follows a strict docket, which controls the time allowed for each part of the discussion, and allows for the assumptions of appropriate roles by members of the group. In the following descriptions I have shown the time docketed, the roles played, and the tasks of the group at each point in the discussion.

Time: 5 minutes.
Task: Clarification of information.

The group may ask the presenter questions of information. The leader firmly resists attempts of the group to begin analysis or evaluation. The point is to provide an occasion for members of the group, on the basis of their study of the case, to ask for additional information and clarification. One of the critical issues for professionals is to learn what they need to know in order to do what they need to do. This part of the docket forces the group to discriminate between information that is interesting and information that is critical. The leader stops the questioning after five minutes and turns the group to its next task.

Time: 25 minutes.
Task: Analysis of dynamics in event.

The presenter becomes timekeeper for the group and cannot participate actively in the discussion. This is, of course, frustrating to presenters. They think of all sorts of things they should have put in the case. The group wants to ask further questions. This is ruled out by the leader as the group concentrates on analysis. The main function of the leader is to guide discussion, keep the group from jumping too quickly to evaluation, and force them to clarify their understanding of the dynamics of the event. I often use a technique I call "unfolding the event": a quick recapitulation of the "description" after clarifying the important background factors. The task of the discussants at this point is to clarify the issues, identify turning points and critical factors, and lay the foundation for serious evaluation. At the end of 25 minutes it is the task of the presenter to call "time," and the leader turns the group to evaluation.

Time: 10 minutes.
Task: Evaluation of performance.

The leader now presses the discussants to make professional evaluations of the practice of the presenter. The evaluation has two parts. The first task is to evaluate professional competence. The basic questions are: Did this person do what he or she set out to do? How well was it done? What, if anything, could this person have done that would have made any difference? If presenters offer any self-evaluation in the written case, we begin with those evaluations. This forces presenters to clarify their objectives and, in future cases, to state them. If presenters don't know what they set out to do, they will never know what they have accomplished! The second task is to assess theological adequacy. The critical questions are: Was this worth doing, or was it worth all the time and effort it took to do it? At this point theological norms, historical traditions, social needs, and so forth, become critical. What is at stake is the adequacy of the action in relation to the nature of the church, the meaning of ministry, the hierarchy of needs and values of persons and society. The group might decide that the minister did a beautiful job, accomplishing all that was set out to do, but that the task was not necessary or valid or worth the time and effort it took. Here the conflicting demands on the pastor are sorted out, priorities are called into question or affirmed, and the group seeks to help the presenter clarify the nature of his or her professional commitment. The presenter again performs the task of timekeeper and calls the group to the next item on the docket.

Time: 10 minutes.
Task: Reflection and reaction by presenter.

The presenter now has opportunity to feedback to the group and to respond to their discussion. I suggest the following questions: At what points was the analysis and evaluation of the group most helpful? What has the group still failed to see and understand? What questions would the presenter like the group to address if it had more time?

Time: 10 minute break before the next case

The leader declares the session adjourned. If the group is discussing several cases at a case conference, the leader will call them back together at the end of the break, introduce the next presenter, and begin the discussion of another case according to the docket. Thus, in a one-hour period, concentrating on a one-page case, a group of from three to twelve ministers address an event in professional practice under this form of the case method. This much information should give a group enough to get started.

Case Studies

A. Leadership, Administration, And Finances
   Cases 1-11

B. Discipleship, Education, And Outreach
   Cases 12-23

C. Counseling And Relationships
   Cases 24-34

1. What Makes A Member?

I serve as pastor of Whitefield Methodist Church, a congregation of 375 members. We are located in a midwestern city of 50,000 people.

"Hello, Pastor, this is Fred Frank calling." So began a conversation which I knew immediately was headed in an unpleasant direction. I was right. "Say, I noticed in the newsletter that Judy's name had been taken off the roll at the Church Conference meeting. How did that happen?" I explained that his daughter had been listed as inactive at the previous two Church Conferences and that, in accordance with the Discipline, her name was removed since she had not responded to the two letters I sent her earlier in the fall. Actually, I lucked out on this encounter because after the meeting Judy had in fact returned the card requesting retention of her membership. For this reason, and in accordance with the Discipline, she was listed as "Restored" and therefore still a member. Learning that, Fred seemed satisfied. He was assured that his 26-year-old unmarried daughter, firmly ensconced in a career in Florida, was still a member of Whitefield.

This conversation highlighted for me the perennial problem of calling folks to be honest with their church membership, while still not offending those who do not share my understanding of this issue.

Every fall I send a letter to all our non-resident members, excluding those in college and in the military. I ask them to respond on a stamped return card whether they want their membership maintained, terminated, or transferred. I encourage them to give serious attention to the latter. Those not responding are listed in the annual meeting minutes as inactive and, after two such prior listings, are recommended for removal.

The main problem arises with parents such as Fred who cannot seem to bear the thought that their child might no longer be interested in organized religion. The usual response of these parents is, "What is their share of the Conference apportionment? I'll pay it and then it won't be costing us anything to keep them on the roll."

When afforded the opportunity, I try to point out that we really aren't doing these people any favor by allowing them to think they have a meaningful relationship to God when it indeed demands nothing of them. Beyond that, it is for me a compromising of the integrity of our membership vows in which we are to support the church with "our prayers, our presence, our gifts, and our service." Nevertheless, there is the pastoral dimension to be considered. When I talked with Judy when she was home a year ago, she indicated some desire to move back home among us if a job became available. Have I completely eliminated the possibility of her being a part of Whitefield congregation by what might seem to be an excessively judgmental action? And what about her father's involvement here? Does that make a difference? Should it?

Focus Questions

1. What are appropriate goals, spiritually and practically, for updating the membership roll as this pastor is doing?

2. How would you evaluate this pastor's procedure in dealing with inactive members who have relocated?

3. Where do you find "grace" and "discipline" in this situation? Are they found where they are needed?

4. How does the judicatory's gathering of membership statistics and basing apportionments on these affect the pastor's and the congregation's actions?

2. The Letter

Abe and Eve are long-time members of St. Paul's Lutheran Church, a 450-member rural congregation in the Midwest. Upon my arrival as pastor, they were regular worshipers but were not involved in other church activities. Their daughter Candy was a teenager and in my confirmation class. Abe and Eve were very friendly toward me and, on one occasion, invited me to their home for dinner. We talked late into the night. They spoke well of the congregation but said they "were not power people" there. Often when I would see Abe and Eve later, they would compliment me on my work and say, "The people at St. Paul's are in love with you." Following Candy's confirmation, she no longer came to church. Within a year she had dropped out of our high school and, at age sixteen, was married. Candy and her husband Joe presently farm with Abe and Eve.

Two years ago, a letter was mailed to Candy expressing concern that she had not communed since confirmation. The letter did not express judgment, but rather conveyed concern for her spiritual life. Abe and Eve have also dropped out of the congregation's life, except to attend funerals. Since Abe is school board president, I see him often and he continues to be friendly.

About eighteen months ago, St. Paul's decided to arrange for a photo directory. Abe and Eve were phoned by our secretary to have their photo taken. An explosion followed. Abe told the secretary they didn't want their picture taken and said the church should be doing other things and not wasting time on picture-taking. He also complained about the letter Candy had received, "kicking her out of the church."

Word got back to me of Abe's complaints. Deciding to use the direct approach, I went to visit Abe and Eve but phoned first. When I arrived, Eve let me in. I sat down at the table and she proceeded to put her hair in rollers. She didn't say much. Later, Abe came in from the barn, fixed us coffee, and we talked for two hours. I told Abe and Eve they had been missed at church for some time. I asked if I had offended them or hurt them in any way, or if the congregation or a member had done so. The response was no.

After pursuing it further, Eve spoke up and asked, "How come the church helped the Newsomes when they lost their farm and even gave them a free place to live, and when the Townleys lost their farm, the church did nothing?" I told her I didn't know the Townleys had lost their farm, and I expressed the difficulty with helping someone when you don't know help is needed. I asked for forgiveness on behalf of the church.

The letter sent to Candy was then mentioned. Anticipating this would happen, I brought a copy of the letter with me. I showed it to them. When they saw the actual contents of the letter, they knew their daughter had not been "kicked out" of the congregation. Again, however, I asked for forgiveness if the congregation had hurt them in any way. Before leaving, I again reminded them that I had missed them at church, and because I cared about them, I hoped they would join us again for worship. I said our family of faith was incomplete without them. To date, none of the four family members has been back to church.

As I weigh this situation, I regard letters as a tool to communicate with members when home visits are not possible, often due to a pastor's hectic schedule. Letters are less personal, however, and as in this case can easily be misinterpreted. Talking about people's inactivity in the church is difficult. People like Abe and Eve just expected me to "know" why they were angry, and it was hard to get them to express their feelings. My sense is that their anger goes much deeper than they expressed to me. I wonder if there is not a power struggle at play, since Abe is a power person in the community but not in the congregation. The challenge will be to probe the situation further. However, I must be honest about my intentions for pursuing this. What ought my goal to be? Is the goal of visits to "inactives" like Abe and Eve to "get them back" in church? If so, why? Is it for my personal satisfaction and accomplishment, or is it out of honest concern for their spiritual well-being?

As a pastor, when I hear rumblings going on within the congregation, it usually seems most expedient to go directly to the source and test out what has been heard. I attempted to do that with Abe and Eve. I offered them a listening ear, even if I didn't get to the root of their anger. That will take more time. I do feel that I have done what I can at this point and have asked for forgiveness on behalf of the congregation. What they do with that is up to them. As much as I would like them to be part of our family of faith again, I realize that I cannot make that happen. I cannot be God. Perhaps now I must simply let God be God.

Focus Questions

1. Letters are a tool of pastoral communication. Consider their usefulness in this situation and others like it. Are their limitations too great here to be useful at all?

2. What are the critical issues here for the pastor to recognize and deal with?

3. What might be more effective alternatives to letters in this situation?

4. Consider the pastor's last lines to "let God be God" in this circumstance. What might be other faithful ways of responding besides this one?

3. Baptism And Community

I came to this 1,100-member midwestern Lutheran congregation one year ago with a long-standing concern for the practice of Baptism in the Lutheran Church. Specifically, I have been concerned that the context of Baptism, basically the home of the child, be a context of faith, not merely tradition. For about twelve years and in two different parishes, I have practiced a form of baptismal counseling or education. At the time I interviewed for the pastorate here, I shared with the Call Committee my practice regarding Baptism. They were genuinely interested. They said on several occasions that there were "a lot of people who used the church for baptisms and weddings and funerals, but wanted nothing else to do with it." It seemed we shared a common concern.

At my first meeting of the Church Council, I shared with them several basic pieces of ministry which I intended to put into place immediately if they would give me their support. One of them was pre-baptismal counseling. I shared my background in this and my concern that Baptism is "initiation into the life of the Christian community" and that it is important that a genuine beginning take place. Here is what I wrote in summary, which they accepted. "When parents request Baptism for their child, they are asked to pick up at the church office a brief cassette and study materials to work with at home. Then, when they have done this, they call the pastor for an appointment to discuss Baptism and what it involves. If they are ready to make the promises Baptism involves, *then* we schedule the Sacrament for their child. Ordinarily and with very few exceptions, Baptisms take place at a worship service of the congregation. Also, the Baptism of a child of non-members would be extremely rare because Baptism assumes that the child and his/her parents will be active members of the church."

In the year thus far, I have baptized sixteen children in the congregation, all of them children where at least one parent was a member. Only three Baptisms took place outside the regular worship service. All parents went through the baptismal counseling procedure with me. However, the low- or no-commitment style Baptism is so prevalent here that my approach will probably make but a dent in "the problem." I think parents are prepared to go through the counseling simply to get what they want, namely Baptism, and then go right on with life as before. (Checking records, out of our 25 parents-of-baptized children in my first year here, only seven communed more than three times — and four did not commune at all. Furthermore, out of 1,100 baptized members of this congregation at mid-year, ninety of them were children — under age ten, mostly under age five — whose parents are members neither of our congregation nor probably any other.)

What I have been doing is just a first step. It may make a difference over a long period of time, but, I believe, not without additional discipline. Recently, when I have been approached for infant Baptism by parents who haven't been worshiping, I basically have said, "Let me see you in church regularly for the next two to three months and then we will talk about Baptism." I expect to be having some intense conversations.

Focus Questions

1. What does the pastor believe to be the basic issues involved here?

2. What are possible effects of such a change in baptismal practice and policy?

3. Are there other ways to include the congregation in this change besides getting the verbal support of leadership?

4. Sometimes how pastors are perceived is part of reality. What are possible perceptions of this pastor?

5. What gains and losses might be expected from the pastor's course of action?

4. Renewal Through Leadership Change

Over the course of time, a small rural Presbyterian congregation of eighty members, located in a southeastern state, had developed a power structure reflective of the community and its families. These powers were essentially backward-looking, status quo, and attentive to self needs, and as such were hindering the progress of the congregation. Procedures and programs of the denomination were affected, as were the spiritual and physical growth of the congregation. This all produced feelings of helplessness, apathy, resentment, and hostility, resulting in a lack of commitment to God, the church, and one another.

After a year in this pastorate, I began to realize the situation and began to look for a way to change it. I strongly felt that a change in leadership was needed and began to explore the rotary system of church officers. I talked with the denominational person responsible for officer training, received material, and studied it. Then I spoke with a pastor who had experienced this system in former pastorates. We discussed the strengths and weaknesses of the two systems, various combinations of them, the official way of instituting the system, and a strategy of presentation.

At the next meeting of the Session when the officers were complaining about their leadership roles and the tiresome burden and frustration of their responsibilities, I presented the idea of the rotary system as a way of relief and a way to involve more people in the congregation. There followed a long and favorable discussion centering on the information about and advantages of a rotary system. The result was that the Session asked me to present a specific plan of implementation for further discussion. I did so. The only objection came from the person representing the power structure who was — providentially, I wonder — absent from the previous meeting. His objection was met with the response, "Let the congregation decide."

A congregational meeting was called for one month later. During the coming month, I carefully explained during the Sunday service the issues involved. I spoke with people individually, maintaining an impartial stance in the presentation. When the meeting came, the congregation took its time. It heard objections from those in power. It listened to the Clerk of Session, who presented it as having the Session's approval (five votes of six) and as having an investment in seeing it passed. In the end, the congregation voted to approve the new system.

What have been the results? Let me list them. (1) In the process, the official leaders began leading, facilitated by the pastor, and they continued to do so afterward. (2) Because of a three-year rotation, six new people were brought into leadership positions, broadening and balancing the power base. For many of the newly elected, their inclusion was a long overdue recognition of years of service. (3) Follow-up training for new officers resulted in more effective leadership. (4) More open and honest communication and expression of ideas began to occur in meetings of church leaders. (5) The congregation became more Presbyterian in policy, procedure, and program. (6) There is evidence of increased involvement and commitment among members of the congregation. (7) Congregational needs began to be met, for example, the much needed and long discussed but previously stymied construction of a church school building.

I want to emphasize that much of this activity was done through the initiative of the members of the congregation, sometimes but not always at the suggestion of the pastor. With the installation of the rotary system of church officers, change has begun to affect all areas of church life and has given them a "new direction" quality.

Focus Questions

1. What do you understand to be key factors in the success of the change initiated by this pastor?

2. What potential roadblocks could the pastor or the congregation have faced but apparently did not? What might have been the response?

3. Are there any fallout issues from this situation which the pastor should be aware of in the future?

5. The Price Of The Dinner

About fourteen months ago when I came to Aldersgate Methodist Church, a typical middle-class, white congregation of 480 members located in our midwestern industrial city of 75,000, I noticed immediately the lack of a fellowship group for adults. I identified a key couple in their middle thirties and asked them to try to pull together a group or reactivate the group which had faded out of existence a couple years ago. At my suggestion the first meeting was a board game night at their house. Three and one-half couples attended! We apparently had not found the key to success.

Bill and Nancy planned the next event, which was to be a "Mystery Dinner" at a local restaurant — at $35 a plate! Obviously, my wife and I were expected to attend. We had two problems with that. First, we almost never spend that much money on an evening's entertainment, and especially for little more than a glorified meal at a restaurant with mixed reviews for its food. Second, we felt we wanted to make a statement about the inappropriateness of our one and only fellowship group's scheduling an activity which excluded a good portion of the younger and/or less affluent members of the congregation.

I decided the best course of action was to explain to Bill and Nancy right up front what our problems were. Their response seemed to be, "Well, we all have to make choices, and if that's your choice, fine." Eighteen people signed up for the evening. One of the older widows approached us after church and offered to pay our way. We declined, explaining that it wasn't just lack of cash that was keeping us away. The issue became moot when the restaurant went bankrupt shortly before our event!

The leaders of the group then decided to have dinner at a much less expensive restaurant, and my wife and I participated in that event, which was well attended.

A bowling evening followed, and after that, a trip to major league baseball game. We did not have to make a decision on the latter because we were on vacation at the time.

Currently, reservations are being solicited for an October date for the local dinner theater's production of *Singing in the Rain,* another $70-plus evening. "Well, Pastor, can we put you and Jane on the list?" Our answer again was "No," but this time it took no explaining. As a matter of fact, I was never approached directly. Bill asked Jane.

I see this as a matter of economic insensitivity resulting from "the good life" for many in our healthy, if not booming, local industrial economy. Apparently, there are a number of folks in the congregation who routinely put out fifty bucks for an evening's entertainment and see nothing inappropriate with scheduling that kind of activity in the name of the church.

A second issue here is how Jane and I make an effective witness on the issue of personal stewardship. Part of the bind is that many of these same people know I have a part ownership in an airplane, an endeavor perceived by many as being a relatively cash-hungry lark.

So, do I continue to decline politely, or do I make a more public statement?

Focus Questions

1. Do you agree with the pastor's assessment of the critical issues here?

2. Apparently the fellowship group leadership did not feel judgment in the pastor's response, nor did it seem to harm his relationships. Why?

3. The witness made by the pastor was important to him. What are the theological and leadership issues? What was or still may be the cost to him?

6. Dissatisfied Members

I serve a midwestern Lutheran congregation of 700 baptized members in a town of 2,000. At first I simply thought the family's absence had been part of the summer slump until someone else also mentioned it to me. I immediately sensed that I needed to follow up on their absence because it was such an abrupt change in behavior and because, three years earlier, I had discouraged the use of pre-recorded accompaniment by soloists. This had been an unhappy decision with the young woman in this family of four (father, mother, two young children).

I met with this couple after they cancelled my first appointment at their home. This time they came to my office, by their request, working between their split shifts on the job. I began by relating to them that I had missed them and I wanted to understand what was happening with them at this time. They proceeded to tell me that they were unhappy with both the Lutheran Church and me as their pastor. Specifically, they didn't like the Lutheran liturgy and I was "not meeting their spiritual needs" — although, they added more than once, they were not saying they were "superior." She had always seemed the stronger person of the two, but he did most of the speaking in our conversation and she deferred to him. It seemed planned. He said that they wanted preaching where he (they? I wondered) felt "convicted," and when I asked for an example, she took the Bible I offered and used Romans 8:1, "There is ... no condemnation for those who are in Christ Jesus." She said, for instance, that I could speak about what "no condemnation" means, and he added that I could preach on who is condemned. She had been on this theme before — "shock 'em into their need for salvation," I call it — and it's always struck me as odd because she's such a "sweet-Jesus" sentimentalist. Furthermore, I should be telling people what to do, specifically what was expected of them, a challenge. He said, "I need to be challenged." I asked later in the conversation if things had gone better with the previous pastor than with me; but no, they had not liked his preaching either. He'd been their pastor almost four years, the same as I have. Besides, they added, they felt kind of forced to join our congregation eight years ago because of friends who've since moved away. Had they found another church? I inquired. Yes, they were attending a Baptist church in the neighboring town where their children had been in a special children's weekday ministry program for a couple years. They indicated nothing would change their mind about staying. I explained briefly a few things about why I was doing my ministry as I was, and I concluded the session by expressing my best wishes for them and their spiritual well-being. He said he appreciated our meeting so he didn't have to feel uncomfortable every time he saw me.

I think one of the main purposes of our meeting was closure. Their minds were made up before we talked and there probably was nothing I could do about that. I was tempted to debate a few theological points but resisted the urge. In spite of my personal feelings that somehow I should have done better in my ministry to them, this decision appears almost inevitable for two reasons: 1) they weren't really sure they should have joined eight years ago, and 2) they had always seemed more Baptist than Lutheran in their expressions of faith. There's a lot of the latter in this congregation, and that sometimes makes me feel like a misfit. At the same time, I find myself thinking about my preaching in relation to their needs.

Focus Questions

1. Had this pastor possibly failed these members, or is he correct in his determination that this is a theological issue, not a pastoral one?

2. Was the pastor too quick to give up on this family as members?

3. Consider how power was being used in this situation.

4. What was at stake here for the several parties involved?

7. Wrong Number

Ronald is a mildly retarded, single male in his mid-fifties. His father served as Bethel Baptist's custodian for over thirty years and Ronald worked with him. The last two years Ronald has worked as a bank custodian while continuing part-time at the church. Bethel is located in a city of 35,000 in a Great Lakes state. Two hundred attend Sunday worship.

Ronald's parents both have died and his sister lives in another state. I assumed his power of attorney four years ago. In this capacity I basically handle Ronald's finances and help guide his decisions.

One aspect of Ronald's character which has come to concern me is an area of sexuality. Ronald literally has thousands of copies of pornographic literature in his apartment, he attends X-rated movies, and recently he has expended large sums of his money calling sexually-oriented 900 telephone numbers.

For a number of months, I have tried to help him understand how the 900 numbers are an attempt to make money and exploit people. Since he continued to make calls and spend large sums of money on them, I decided to call the telephone company and put a "block" on his phone so that he could not call 900 numbers. I did not tell Ronald that I put the block on his phone and he has never mentioned anything about it.

Ronald has the body of an adult but the mind of an adolescent. He seems to think that these girls on the telephone really care about him and that he has a chance of meeting them, maybe even marrying or at least finding companionship. In addition, Ronald has a communication problem with people. He rarely shares his true feelings with others. When I speak with him about the 900 numbers, he agrees and seems to understand; yet his actions continue unchanged.

I know that I am doing the responsible thing by not allowing Ronald to waste so much of his money on the 900 numbers. I do feel, however, that I need to find a way to tell him why he is not able to call these numbers any longer. My fear is that he will call the phone company and arrange to remove the block. The deeper struggle within me has to do with Ronald's freedom and how much authority I claim in his life as his power of attorney.

———

Focus Questions

1. To what extent are the critical issues of this case personal and not professional?

2. How do you see the needs in Ronald's life, and what is the pastor's role in meeting them?

3. What is an appropriate use of power here?

8. The Exception

Mrs. Turillo, a woman in her early fifties, is a wife, mother of four, and a full-time employee at a nursing home in a nearby community. She has raised two of her four children, with two still at home. This family lives in the country across the road from another member family actively involved in our 400-member rural midwestern Lutheran congregation. Upon my arrival as pastor of this congregation, the Turillo family was very friendly toward me. The daughter, then a sixth grader, took a real liking to me. Every Sunday she would make comments about the fine sermons I preached.

One early October morning, I was out of my office when a phone call came from Mrs. Turillo. I returned the call shortly thereafter. The purpose of her initial call was to ask if her daughter could begin confirmation instruction when she was in seventh grade rather than the usual eighth grade. She said it would be more convenient for them, because then she and the neighbors' son could come together. I told her I would consider her request and give her an answer later.

I decided a request like this could best be handled at a church council meeting. That way the final decision would be off my shoulders and on the leadership of the congregation. At the next council meeting I explained the request without using names. I expressed to the council why I did not support the request. Council members discussed the situation at length and decided confirmation instruction should continue to begin in eighth grade — no exceptions. Our congregation includes in its monthly newsletter, mailed to all members, a summary of council actions. Thus when Mrs. Turillo read the newsletter, she would be informed of the decision made. I failed to contact Mrs. Turillo immediately. In fact, I didn't contact her until months later, having decided to wait until closer to the next fall's instruction time.

Word came back to me via church members that Mrs. Turillo was furious with me. She was angry that I had taken her request to the council rather than making the decision on my own. In addition, the fact that I had failed to respond personally to her request until much later made her more unhappy. She began bad-mouthing me to many people. She began coming to church only occasionally. When she was present, she seemed inattentive, talked during my sermons, and refused to shake my hand at the door. Her daughter began behaving in similar ways. At one point the chaplain of the nursing home where Mrs. Turillo works asked me about my relationship with her. He said she had expressed her anger toward me with him and had commented, "I don't think my daughter will go to hell if she isn't confirmed. I don't think I'll send her to class."

Some time later, Mrs. Turillo entered the hospital for major surgery. I went to visit her. After brief conversation to determine how she was feeling, I confronted her with my concern about our relationship. I reflected on her family's warm reception of me when I first became their pastor, and also on the present time with rather hostile feelings surfacing. I expressed concern that her daughter's attitude toward me had changed, too, and I had not even spoken directly with her. I asked what prompted the change. Mrs. Turillo responded with her own complaints, and I then asked her forgiveness. I conveyed my desire to be on friendly terms with her again.

Let me reflect on this situation. Mrs. Turillo was not granted her wish to have her daughter attend confirmation early. She was unhappy that I felt a need to consult the council about her request. Due to our differing understandings as to what is proper procedure, conflict occurred. She felt that I handled the situation poorly. Her way of dealing with me was to make my life difficult by bad-mouthing me to others.

My first mistake was to delay my response to Mrs. Turillo. I ought to have informed her immediately of the church council decision, rather than have her read it in the church newsletter. When word got back to me that she was angry and talking negatively to others about me, I became frustrated, angry at myself, and upset with Mrs. Turillo for her behavior. It seemed only right, however, that I apologize to her and express my desire to mend our relationship. I did that, and things seem better between us. Her daughter has been a good student in confirmation class. I still sense, however, that Mrs. Turillo is somewhat unhappy with me. It may be time for another heart-to-heart talk.

Focus Questions

1. The pastor clearly identifies one pastoral mistake — a delayed response to Mrs. Turillo — and apologizes to her for this. Do you concur that this pastoral apology was needed and appropriate?

2. The perception of how this matter should have been handled in the first place varied with pastor and parishioner. The latter thought the pastor should decide, the former thought the council should. Could the roots of the problem be here? How might this misunderstanding have been prevented?

3. How is power being used by the parties in this matter?

4. Mrs. Turillo is still unhappy. If you were the pastor calling on her, what would you want to be attentive to?

9. The New Roof

Mr. and Mrs. Kent are lifelong members of Tall Oak Methodist, an eighty-family congregation in our midwestern town of 2,600. The family membership of Mr. Kent can be traced back to the congregation's founding more than 130 years ago. He has been a church leader and takes great pride in recounting the number of souls he has won for the Lord. He is a very gruff-sounding and stern-looking man, and he has probably scared off as many souls as he has won. Both Kents are past the 75-year mark. Mr. Kent has become the only living person who knows all the tricks to taking care of the physical operation of the church, but he's very slow in passing this knowledge on to others.

It happens that the church roof had a flat section which was in very poor condition. The congregation decided it should be removed and replaced with a slanted roof. Mr. Kent, who is no longer a trustee at his own request, entered my office and demanded to know who was going to oversee the roof project. I assured him that the trustees would be taking care of everything, since I happened to be committed to an out-of-town mission retreat during the week the roof was scheduled to be repaired.

I returned Saturday evening to find the project completed and the grounds all cleaned up. Sunday morning, as I was preparing to enter the sanctuary for worship, Mr. Kent pulled me aside and told me in no uncertain terms that the trustees had not done a thing. The only reason anything was done, he continued, was because he did it "all by himself." I was angry and upset. I had a miserable worship thinking that there really was no commitment from these newer, younger trustees.

Later I discovered that the new trustees had come to church after work and found that nothing needed to be done. It turns out that retired Mr. Kent had been there all day, every day, and had completed his supervision while the trustees were away at work. The trustees thought that the construction crew had done all the work. They didn't realize Mr. Kent had been there until I began asking questions about why they didn't do anything.

I believe that Mr. Kent, out of good intentions, wanted to see that the work was done properly. His naturally aggressive personality led him to do more than necessary. He then became bitter and directed his anger toward me, as part of that visible target of newer and younger church leadership.

Although Mr. Kent had taken himself formally off the trustees, he had not handed over the reins to "the new kids." His experience was proof, in his mind, that they weren't willing or able really to do it anyway.

I also think that for him to admit that someone else can handle the tasks he used to do would mean that he feels he has no worth to the church. My frustration is that I'm not sure how to address this with him. My suspicion is that he would react strongly that this is not the case, and his personal proof would be the fact that it was by his own request that he was no longer a trustee.

I feel that I handled the situation poorly. I was angry with the new trustees for being irresponsible, then with Mr. Kent for misleading me. There had been indications which should have tipped me off prior to this event. Mr. Kent was very often in my office when I first arrived, pointing out what should be done here and there. I took this as helpfulness, but now I see those frequent visits as other ways Mr. Kent was controlling the actions of the trustees via my office.

I still have a great deal of frustration with Mr. Kent. I find myself being short and impatient with him whenever he visits me. I'd prefer to relax with him instead of catching myself in a personal power struggle with him.

Focus Questions

1. The transition of power from one group or generation to another can be very painful, both personally and institutionally. Describe what Mr. Kent and the new congregational leadership may be feeling.

2. What do Mr. Kent and the congregation need?

3. What might be an appropriate goal for the pastor to adopt at this time?

4. What could the pastor do to accomplish this goal?

10. The Unhappy Employee

Let me describe a situation at the time I arrived at Zion Lutheran Church, a congregation of 750 in a large midwestern city.

Frieda, our music program director, was recovering from a cracked kneecap, the result of a fall at church. Her duties were being done marginally. When she came back to work, she often complained to me about how much work she had to do and told about how close she was to the former pastor. This pastor had died suddenly at the age of fifty years.

At first, I tried just to encourage Frieda, pointing out things I would like to see her doing. She began to resent my suggestions and would say that things weren't the same around here anymore. She complained about her pay, saying that the church wasn't appreciating all that she did.

At one point, I suggested to her that if she wasn't happy here, she should feel free to explore another job. I told her that I really didn't want to go on hearing her complaints, that it wasn't good for her or the congregation to have her so unhappy.

One day Frieda's best friend called and asked to see me. She said she had a very unhappy friend since I became pastor here. She said that I was too demanding, and that she would not want to work for me. She had suggested to Frieda that she find other work, but it was not easy in this job market. She also reported Frieda's underlying commitment to the church and said, "There isn't anything Frieda wouldn't do for you if she knew you appreciated her work. She loves this congregation and hates to leave many of the people she serves here." At the end of this session I promised to have a good, frank discussion with Frieda, affirming her as a person and trying to work out an attainable work plan with her so she might experience more success.

The next week Frieda and I had a heartfelt talk, with both of us expressing our desire to work things out. We agreed to set up a weekly session, planning her work in some detail. I promised to "go to bat" to get her more pay when the Board of Personnel proposed salaries for the coming year.

From that time on Frieda's attitude has been better. She still has a tendency to complain at times, but she generally is in a good frame of mind. She eventually suggested that we get the whole staff together once a week to plan our work. She has felt affirmed by seeing her idea carried out.

Over the four years we've been together, I've begun to appreciate Frieda's really outgoing love for the people of the congregation and for our whole staff. She still does not do some things as well as I would like at times, but she is doing a better job. I've found that she responds much better to honest praise than she did to pointing out what she should do. In fact, I'm very careful not to criticize her but always surround my suggestions with expressions of appreciation.

I still wonder at times about how we could do a better job with our music program, but I am content that we are making some progress. Our relationship is now stable and genuinely friendly.

Focus Questions

1. What are Frieda's issues and needs? What is the meaning of things "not (being) the same around here anymore"?

2. The time frame is that of a pastoral start-up. How does that impact what the pastor did — or might have done — in this situation?

3. A concern for the whole person is demonstrated by the pastor who, in the process, sacrifices some job performance in the staff member's role. Discuss this trade-off and the church role in those business decisions.

11. The Pastor Must Go!

Pastor Michael has been actively leading congregations for nearly ten years. All have been theologically mainline, rural congregations under 200 members. These congregations have seen modest reactivation of inactive members plus increases in giving and membership under his leadership. Two years ago, Pastor Michael was sent to an aggressively evangelical Methodist congregation in the Midwest. It, too, has fewer than 200 members and is located in a town of 3,000. This was the first time Pastor Michael would follow a very popular pastor.

On a particular Friday afternoon recently, Pastor Michael received a phone call from his District Superintendent saying that four of his church members had just called on him. They were troubled about the major reduction in church funds, the loss of members, a great drop in giving, and a future mass exodus of strong church members. Pastor Michael was instructed by the D.S. to "sit tight" through the weekend until Tuesday when the whole group would meet with him and express their concerns. The thrust of Friday's meeting had been that "Pastor Michael must go!" Many of the facts presented by the group were distorted half-truths. Pastor Michael had been aware of constant murmurings, but these were never put forward. They were provided almost always as second-hand information.

Pastor Michael's wife had recently been promoted to a supervisory position at work. His children are young and have experienced school only in the current system. He and his family like the school, the community, and several members of the congregation. Now Pastor Michael is feeling he must stay and work out this problem, regardless of whether the problem is really his or not. After all, it has been his career which has caused his family to be moved away from successful work and friendships at other times, too.

It seems that Pastor Michael is deciding to work on resolving the problem no matter what the cost. His main goal had been keeping his family here for a period longer than five years. Now he questions whether it's going to be worth it. Could this trouble be the working of the Holy Spirit so that he might be moved to another church which might flourish under his style of leadership? Or was this a mismatch from the beginning? Should he not worry about his family but simply relieve his own stress by allowing the system to reappoint him to a new location? His spouse has indicated that she will understand.

As things stand, Pastor Michael is far from being out of the woods. He understands that his present course of action — staying no matter what — means many compromises on his part. This may open up a new line of communication with the grumblers. This in turn may quiet them, a fact of no small importance since they represent a small but potentially powerful segment of the congregation. It is still possible that his denominational leaders may choose to move him, and then the situation would be out of his control.

———

Focus Questions

1. Describe the power dynamics you see at work here.

2. If this is a pastor-congregation mismatch, what resources are available to Pastor Michael and his family?

3. How might Pastor Michael approach ministry with the group of malcontents, knowing that they approach faith and life so differently from him?

4. What are Pastor Michael's spiritual needs at this time? How might he tend to them?

12. The Confirmation Challenge

Our congregation has used an individualized confirmation instruction for ten years. We are a 1,500-member Lutheran congregation in a Plains state town of 10,000. This confirmation approach has meant that around fifty eighth and ninth graders meet from 3:30 to 6:00 p.m. each Wednesday after school to study and discuss materials of traditional Lutheran confirmation content. The individualized methodology means that they study in configurations of one to five students, using a variety of audio-visual materials: books, Bibles, filmstrips, cassettes, videos, and so forth. Students study in one of about fifteen classrooms on two floors in the education unit. They are supervised by a person who makes appointments for them with a pastor when they are ready, plus a monitor on each floor who okays memory work. Students are required to complete sixteen packets or units in two years, about one a month. To complete a packet and move on to the next, in a small group they must have a satisfactory discussion on the assignment with one of the pastors. All work toward the same May confirmation date through the two years, although theoretically they could complete their work in less time.

Although the program has been fine-tuned and some material revised each year, the program seemed to have an abundance of difficulties. The students seemed to adopt a kind of party atmosphere to the after-school gathering, conversing more and studying less. They often copied worksheet answers directly from each other, without ever doing the work, even though they were told that was dishonest and unacceptable. They were generally less disciplined and more inclined to make the monitors' work difficult.

At the beginning of the school year, I had tried to inform students and parents of these concerns through our usual orientation meeting and with a note mailed home about a month later. It did not change things. About three months into the year, I informed the students I would occasionally use a quiz format within the discussion periods. Several of them, including good students, were upset about this, and we spoke about it at length. All this was going on while my pastor-colleague was abroad, and a pastor from overseas was my partner in hearing unit discussions with the students. He was concerned with similar matters, including a lack of comprehension of the materials covered.

When my pastor-colleague returned halfway through the year, I told him of the situation and that I was ready to try another approach. We conversed about this, he spoke to the students when my family and I vacationed for two weeks, and I would say we "slugged it through" to the year's end. He saw the difficulties as strongly connected with his absence, but I more with the inadequacies in the program. Both of us agreed something had to be done. We decided on two major changes for the current year: (1) that students would have two twenty-minute discussions for each packet instead of one thirty-minute, and (2) that we would have meetings of the entire class four times during the year. We hope that this will deal with the lack of discipline, at least in part with honesty issues, and also add a community component to the program.

As I look at this, the presence of the overseas pastor was a factor, especially since he wanted less involvement in the congregation's ministry than we had understood. Yet the students were taking advantage of the system. They were seeing themselves too little as a community of learning. In addition, shorter attention spans and increasing personal and family problems were affecting their work. Informing parents did little or nothing to improve the situation. I suspect they did not consider this their problem.

We did "hang on" as best we could through the school year. My own relationship with several youths and parents might have been better if I'd done a better job anticipating the problems. Currently the program seems to be the best it's been in years. Beginning students, as an entire class, are on schedule with their work. A continuing disappointment is the disruptive presence of three second year students who have both learning and personal problems and who are being caught up in their studies by my pastor-colleague. The question remains how best to deal with them and others like them.

———

Focus Questions

1. What does the pastor believe to be the critical issues? Do you agree?

2. Who has the power here and how is it being used?

3. What is at stake here for the congregation and for the pastor?

13. More Than Furnace Heat

Mr. Zull has been a loyal member for more than forty years in this old 75-family Methodist congregation located in a midwestern town. He had been the head usher for the past few years and has served as the chairman of the church trustees for the last one and one-half years. He and his wife have always been supportive of my pastoral leadership.

The church has had a poor furnace set-up for the five years that I have been here. The oil tanks, located in a "lean-to" basement, leak ever so regularly. Nearly everyone notices the "oily" smell, but it's not so bad that you cannot overlook it. The church youth group is the only one to get the full effect of the fumes when they gather in the basement for their meetings and Sunday School. Most of the congregation, however, is somewhat oblivious to the problem. At the same time, we pay for several annual service calls on the furnace. The result is that we've been working for a full year to try to replace the old furnace with efficient gas heat. The subject has been on the agenda at our congregation's annual meeting and several subsequent council meetings. Recently when the trustees met to discuss the furnace situation, I was present and took the minutes of the meeting.

During the trustees' report at the last council meeting, Mr. Zull launched into a tirade. He pointed at me and, with face flushed red, stated, "Here's the bid on the furnace that YOU made me get! It's out of my hands! I didn't want to do this, but here you are!" A shocked and embarrassed council went deadly silent, and everyone turned to look at me! As I sat there on the hot seat, I knew one source of pressure which we all knew: namely, that church finances had been running close to $1,000 short each month. As calmly as I could, I attempted to remind him that this was a congregation-owned project. Silently I wished that someone else would speak up. I was angry and embarrassed. I felt like blowing up in response to him, but I realized this would not be best for my credibility, leadership, or self-worth. I was not going to get suckered into a fight, even though I felt he wanted one right then and there.

As I reflect on that moment, I think it's very possible Mr. Zull had been experiencing some flak from other church members. This congregation has, it should be noted, some very vocal resistance forces. Or perhaps the report of $6,000 in indebtedness, an internal loan, was "the straw that broke the camel's back." As an older member of the congregation, Mr. Zull also may have been responding out of a "Herr Pastor" mindset when his back was up against the wall — meaning, when there's hot water brewing, pour it on someone else in charge, in this case, the pastor. I have never tried to operate the congregation in this way, but some people's feelings about the pastor's role are set early in their life. I try to remember this when dealing with older congregation members. Their expectations about the pastoral role may be different from my own.

I think I acted appropriately. I've learned never to get so wrapped up in leading the congregation that its issues are my issues, and that I am seen as the focal point of the church's purpose and meaning. I have told myself, "Forgive, forgive, forgive," and wait for God to turn things around. Because of Mr. Zull's previous support for me, I was quite sure that this was not a personal attack. Something else — I hope! — had triggered his outburst. In fact, he has continued to communicate with me on the issue, and I have hopes that we all will come out of this okay.

Focus Questions

1. How do you understand Mr. Zull's outburst coming at the pastor "out of the blue"? What might be under the surface?

2. What part may be played in this situation by differing expectations of the pastor?

3. What resources are required by a pastor to respond as this one did?

56

14. The Pastor's Raise

One of the responsibilities of the Pastor-Parish Relations Committee in a United Methodist congregation is to negotiate annually with the pastor regarding compensation, and subsequently, to make a recommendation to the Church Conference, the congregation's annual meeting. Our 400-member rural midwestern congregation in a county seat town has a PPRC of seven members, elected on a three-year rotation. Three members are directly related to farming; the others are a high school student, a preschool teacher, a county office worker, and a power company lineman. At the meeting in question, one farmer and the lineman were absent.

The PPRC meeting was getting long. We had worked through salary levels and budgets for the secretary and custodians. We had reviewed the recommendations of the Music Committee for the musicians' salaries. Finally, time came to discuss my salary, the pastor's. After reviewing for the PPRC the various components of my compensation, designed to minimize taxes, I presented information showing ranking relative to other pastors in our district for similar years of service, size of congregation, and salary (about 45 positions). I presented information regarding the salaries of neighboring Methodist pastors. I gave the committee no clear direction as to my expectations, feeling that struggle on their part is healthier than a simple reaction to the pastor's proposal. Then I left the room.

After what seemed to be an eternity I was called back in and was seated. The chairperson pulled out the budget request sheets which the Finance Committee was asking to be filled out and said, "The figures are: for salary $xxxxx, for health insurance $xxxx," and so on down the line. During what I remember as a very humiliating silence, I grabbed my calculator and began figuring what the amounts were in percentages. What I learned was that this was a raise of approximately one-half the percentage of the Consumer Price Index (CPI). This is far less than I had expected.

I had three courses of action available to me at that point. I could have swallowed hard and said nothing. I could have said, "I find this unacceptable; I'll make you a counter offer, and if you don't look at it seriously, I'll see that there's a counter proposal at the annual meeting." Or I could say, as I did, "I find this well beneath what I had hoped for, but since it is about the minimum established by the Conference, I have little grounds to demand more." I asked for the committee's rationale, to which the chairperson said it reflected the economic situation of the community. After a few housekeeping details, the meeting adjourned.

What was going on in the PPRC, it appears to me, was a power play by the chair who had been critical of my ministry for some time. This was allowed by two others who felt that "if they weren't getting a raise, no one else should either." For me the issue was as much sensitivity to my feelings as it was economics. I was angry that the chairperson did not seem to feel he owed me any more than a simple statement of the numbers; I had to ask to get a rationale.

What else was going on is a real confusion in my own mind about the system of rewards I buy into as motivation for ministry. To what extent, for example, am I "of the world" as well as in it? And power plays aside, how do I handle negotiations in such a way as to make the experience mutually positive rather than win/lose?

Focus Questions

1. What are the key issues as seen by this pastor?

2. Assuming that pastors are truly called to share the life in the community where they live, discuss the validity of the chair's rationale that the pastor's raise reflected the economic situation of the community.

3. Part of the congregation's stewardship is paying a decent wage to their pastor. To what extent do pastors, including this one, become enablers of poor stewardship by quietly accepting low salaries in the interest of balancing the budget?

4. What are the potential gains and losses here?

15. What Can We Cut?

Giving for current fund and benevolence purposes at our 250-member Lutheran congregation, located in a Great Lakes city of 25,000, has been insufficient to meet expenses and obligations. The Council, therefore, encouraged the Finance Committee and Stewardship Committee (this latter actually just one Council person) to meet and decide how to meet the problem.

Whenever this matter has arisen before, the typical reaction of Council and finance people has been, "What shall we cut?" No consideration has been given to increasing giving. Giving within the congregation is what I would consider poor — between two and one-half and three percent of members' income. Stewardship always has been a stepchild to the other great works of the church such as dartball, bowling, and so on. The Stewardship Committee has always had, at best, one or two members.

The second part of the giving problem was that the congregation had decided at its last annual meeting to embark on a driveway and parking lot resurfacing job at a cost of $12,000-15,000 above the current fund, benevolence, and building fund expenses. Last year the parking lot had been expanded and drainage tile put in at a cost of $6,000, an amount raised in special offerings.

Here's what happened. Since the voice of previous financial problems had been heard well and there was nothing left to be cut (except my salary), I decided to try to lead the Finance/Stewardship Committee to consider other alternatives. Prior to the meeting, I spent a couple hours analyzing the problem, studying the force field of negative and positive influences, and establishing some possible goals to reach the overall objective of increased giving. I typed up each step and submitted the proposal to the council membership representing Stewardship. I told him I would like to lead the committee in exploring alternatives such as I had done with this sheet.

Prior to the meeting I also prepared a two-page worksheet which included the following questions: 1) what is the problem, 2) what forces aggravate and/or help the situation, 3) what is the priority of each force, 4) what goals can be set, 5) how are the goals to be reached, and 6) who will do what?

Incredibly, this approach worked! The question of what could be cut was not raised. The committee discussed several different goals, and people volunteered to take responsibility for the outcome. While I would have wished for far more results in terms of a more extensive stewardship awareness effort, nevertheless I am pleased that something is being done. I should add, however, that one goal was a variation of the old cutting question. It involved "robbing Peter to pay Paul" in that, once a month, current fund and benevolence monies would simply be shifted from giving to the building fund.

Obviously one Finance/Stewardship Committee meeting cannot change the low level of stewardship within the congregation. If these financial leaders, however, can at least begin to consider the issues of stewardship, then we may have achieved a bit of success. My sermons of late have dealt quite directly with stewardship and financial matters. While this has been offensive to a few, there has been an increased interest in evangelism. After all, someone said, our costs are fairly fixed and the addition of new members will do nothing but improve the situation!

Focus Questions

1. How would you describe the situation being addressed, in addition to money matters?

2. The pastor describes his own role in a situation where leaders have low investment. How do you analyze his approach, and what alternatives might there be?

3. Even though biblical and theological issues have not been voiced here, what are several key themes? How might they come to bear on the situation?

4. Here, as in many congregations, there are the realities of both the immediate crisis and also the longer term need which may or may not be addressed. How do you see these matters here and respond to them?

16. Between A Rock And A Hard Place

Hope Church is a 200-member Lutheran mission congregation located in a midwestern town of 2,500. Our national church body provides funds for each new congregation for a period of five to seven years on a decreasing basis. The congregation is expected to move toward self-sufficiency by membership growth and increased giving by the members.

Hope has not been growing at the rate we projected. Consequently, giving has not been able to increase at the rate funding has decreased. The situation continues to worsen. Caught between a rock and a hard place, Hope struggles to increase giving and membership. The concern is how to preach the Gospel along with the call to discipleship, the free gift of salvation along with the responsibilities of church membership.

At our most recent council meeting, the treasurer concluded his report by telling us that we were $1,000 in the red. Furthermore, our savings account was depleted, and we were continuing to go deeper in debt at the rate of $1,000 a month. Discussion revolved around ways we could communicate this situation to the congregation. What do we do? Do we have more stewardship sermons by the pastor or more temple talks by laity? Do we write letters or publicize it in the newsletter?

The council, with guidance from the pastor, decided that stewardship is an integral part of the gospel message and would be part of a sermon. It also decided that the needs of the congregation were a matter for the entire membership. A letter would be written, an article would appear in the newsletter, and concern would be shared individually by the council members. Neither temple talks during the worship service nor pleas for money would be made.

In reflecting on this situation, several critical questions come to mind. (1) A common criticism of the institutional church is that it is always out for money. How do we deal with this criticism and concern? (2) What is the balance between the free gift of salvation and the cost of discipleship? Because of financial necessity, the church often pushes growth in stewardship in disproportion to other areas of growth. (3) How does a congregation handle finances in such a way that it does not diminish the joy of the Gospel?

This is an ongoing struggle for the pastor and congregation of Hope Lutheran Church. The pressure of finances tempts us to be law-oriented. So far we have not given in to that temptation. A balance has been struck, but it is an uneasy balance. The pastor constantly questions whether he is too soft on the people or too hard. So far the balance has allowed people to enter into the congregation freely, but currently this is not meeting the congregation's financial needs.

Focus Questions

1. With the congregation's growth being less than projected, what dynamics might you expect to see at work here?

2. The pastor writes of "balance" in his/her messages between Gospel and discipleship, between gift and responsibility. How would you see this?

3. Money issues are often intimately related to the perception of mission as seen by members. What is at stake here?

17. The Interview

"It was a dark and stormy night," and Allen's first question did little to lighten the mood. "Would you please tell us," he asked, "why you left each of your previous employments and what you bring to Bethel which would be different?"

An "Introductory Meeting," that's what the cabinet of Methodist District Superintendents (DS) called these things — an opportunity for the pastor they are intending to appoint to a new congregation to meet with the Staff-Parish Relations Committee (SPRC). The purpose was to find out a bit about each other and set the stage for a smooth transition. This one, taking place in a congregation of 300 in a midwestern city of 60,000, felt like a hostile job interview.

For an hour and a quarter, the questioning continued, mostly from Allen. "What words would the children, aged eight to twelve, use to describe you?" "Obviously the cabinet feels you are uniquely qualified for this position; what do you consider to be your unique qualifications?" A few others asked questions and volunteered information at those occasional opportunities I had to ask questions of them, but for the most part, Allen ran the show.

Finally, Ernie, the DS, said, "Why don't you and your wife step out for a few minutes while I have some words with the committee?" We did. An hour later he came out and said, "Well, they will accept the appointment, but they have some more questions."

My wife and I returned to the meeting and Allen began again. "Well, we really were hoping for someone younger, someone with more charisma and enthusiasm, someone with a record of successes, because success leads to success; but I am willing to give the marriage a try. But if it doesn't work, my family and I are out of here." After a few parting comments, I headed back into the cold, windy night, feeling that I had accepted an appointment to a congregation whose SPRC desperately did not want me.

What do I do now? Initially I intended to contact Allen before I moved to explore further his pain with my appointment. I decided not to do this because I assessed him as a sort of self-appointed power broker and I did not want to legitimize his position. A conversation I had with the DS tended to verify my assessment.

My first Sunday at Bethel Allen was away on a family activity. The next Sunday he was there and all smiles. His family, I learned, was still out of town visiting relatives. I called his home the next week intending to invite him to dinner at our house since he was alone. He was not home and I left a message on the machine. He returned to church the next Sunday, saying that his family was back. He would be glad to get together for lunch sometime, but he was going to be out of town for work much of the next couple weeks.

Since that day, he has been at worship about half the Sundays, and his greetings have been warm. He has, however, missed all three meetings of the SPRC since my coming, always, it seemed, for valid reasons. His absence, I must add, has prevented me from getting any sense of how he is going to operate in that committee now that I am here.

At this point I do not intend to make another overture toward meeting with him, but I would be willing to meet if he were to suggest it.

What do I make of all this? About a week ago, I finally decided to trust my Ministry Assistant who happens to be a good friend of Allen's. I asked what's going on with this guy who gave me all the grief in the meeting. She said she has observed this to be Allen's style on several occasions when he gets upset about an issue. He comes on from a very domineering posture, and then it's over.

"Wherefore Allen's anger?" I asked.

She related the presence of a profound frustration on the part of the SPRC with the DS over the SPRC's inability to get a change in pastoral leadership a year ago. The SPRC perceived that the DS was blaming the congregation for its decline, but they themselves saw the problem as being an ineffective pastor. The DS had asked them to be very careful and specific in their criteria for their new pastor, and it had become clear early on in the process that I did not come close to filling that bill. In their judgment, the cabinet had ignored the SPRC's work and appointed someone who was in trouble with his congregation and needed a new job. In essence, I became the scapegoat that evening for Allen and others to work out their anger against the cabinet.

At this writing, now three months into my move to Bethel, the honeymoon still holds. The Ministry Assistant says that everyone she talks with, that is, everyone who is in a position to make a comparison, says I am not the person they thought they were interviewing. As of now, I am considering this conflict with Allen to be history.

Focus Questions

1. Discerning the truth or reality of a situation often is difficult. Are there other ways the pastor might have discovered the truth or reality behind the anger in this situation?

2. What are the strengths in this pastor's approach to the situation generally and to Allen specifically?

3. Allen came on like a "clergy killer" but apparently was not one. Can a pastor make an accurate initial diagnosis about what he is dealing with, and if so, how?

4. The pastor was never informed of the SPRC's anger toward the DS. Is there unfinished business here?

18. Worship On Tape

About three years ago I came to this 325-family midwestern Lutheran congregation, succeeding a pastor who had been here seventeen years. A brief interim followed him. In the mission statement from the congregation when I was called was: "To renew all church programs such as music, adult education, and fellowship." I knew many aspects of parish life needed work, but the extent to which this was so always amazed me as time went on. I also observed that I was more "high church," though not to an extreme.

One practice which troubled me happened in my first six months here. Several soloists had used taped accompaniment for singing at worship. One of them had asked my opinion, and I'd said I wasn't fond of it, but if he wanted to try it for a time, that was okay. As three to four months passed, two or three other singers simply began using tapes, often with full orchestra, as background. With each successive one, I became increasingly uncomfortable, especially after getting tapes six Sundays in a row. I began to analyze what was happening in me. Part of the discomfort was the Christian "pop" style of music, often very sentimental and very out of harmony with much of the Lutheran musical tradition. Another part was a sense of inappropriateness, hearing orchestra where there was none. And a third part was a conviction that worship of God deserved our best, not "canned" music, but actual live musicians.

I shared my thoughts with organists and choir directors (five people) and they were divided in opinion on the matter. However, I asked them if they objected to my speaking with the soloists individually, thanking them for their music and requesting that they would ordinarily be accompanied by a pianist or other musician, not a tape. They all agreed to this. I proceeded to contact the singers and the matter was ostensibly settled.

In a way, the matter went well as far as I was concerned. A potentially upsetting matter was handled with a minimum of fuss. I have continued to have a good relationship with each of the singers, at least on the surface. However, I suspect they have been far less involved in solo work than they might have been if I had said nothing. One real dilemma is our lack of suitable accompanists, which I recognized at the beginning, too. The other matter is that of preparation time and convenience. Taped background has been used probably only two or three times in the two years since I took this action. I think I would handle this the same if it were to happen again. However, I am disturbed by potentially "putting down" someone's gifts, although that was not my intent and runs counter to my basic convictions. I also am aware this subject touches on an area I might refer to as "standards and tastes." Acting out of my theology and tradition, I don't want to be arbitrary but in such matters as these it's possible to appear that way.

Focus Questions

1. How do you find yourself reacting to the pastor's identification of the critical issues here?

2. What other theological issues are at stake, and how relevant are they?

3. What do you think about the pastor's inclusion of other musicians in the process? What about the role of the council?

4. The issue may be likely to resurface. What can be done to deal with these concerns long term?

19. Depressing Discussions

Mrs. Quell is the treasurer of this rural midwestern Methodist congregation of 150 members. She has had this position for one year prior to my appointment and will continue for a total of four years. She is eligible to be appointed for another four-year term. She also is the chair of the Administrative Council. She has a very aggressive personality. She and her husband are not native to this rural congregation but have been part of it for ten years. The family has settled on their present farm on a permanent basis, and Mrs. Quell is under much pressure because it is her mother's farm. In addition there are numerous family problems with their four adult sons.

When I arrived at the congregation, I informed the Council that I needed two things done for me. One, I needed a secretary, and two, I wanted bulletin covers purchased so I would not have to spend time making them each week. Both requests involved spending money in new areas.

Mrs. Quell's response was, "We don't know how long you'll be working out here." This, by the way, was said the first time I had met the woman. I could sense hostility from her. Since then, there have been other asides made by her, too, such as, "We'd have more money to give to missions if we didn't have to buy bulletins or pay a secretary," and "The books look like Pastor needs to bring in more money." The major confrontation recently came in December when she paid conference expenses and informed me that I had failed to get in enough money to pay my salary or mileage expenses.

I have observed Mrs. Quell and can see how she and her husband can direct the emotional level of a entire Council meeting. If they have a quarrel, this will carry into the meeting. Even when we have a balance of more than $1,000 in the treasury, she can depress everyone's mood by listing the bills that will be coming. I find that I can get depressed just thinking about one of these meetings.

Additional stress comes when we begin to discuss a potential building project. This increases her bitterness. In our discussion

68

of this project, which is a necessity, she can get us all depressed to the point of hopelessness. I feel that Mrs. Quell is a very unhappy person. Her constant need to make everyone else depressed seems to indicate this. I wonder about her inner feelings. She must feel as if she is out of control and thus feels she needs to control others. The more a person feels out of control in one area, the more she feels a need to compensate with extra controls in another area. Mrs. Quell keeps the farm records, and I know that the unknowns of the farming industry and the depressed finances of farming weigh heavily upon her. If she feels lack of control here, she surely is able to control a meeting. Related to these control issues, too, is the fact that she and her husband are among the largest contributors to the congregation.

Other dynamics here are the reality that the pastor possesses authority, as does the taxation system. Perhaps she has no personal gripe with me, but opposes me because of my position as pastor, a position which is fairly new to me. I find myself stressed because I see this as a power struggle, which in reality it might not be.

How do I see this? Rather than interrupting the process in the meetings, I have allowed Mrs. Quell to manipulate my own feelings as well as those of others. Perhaps she needed the opportunity to speak her mind, but then perhaps I should have directed the meeting to hear the feelings of others without aggressiveness toward her. I'd like to make a learning experience out of this, unless that's too idealistic.

What I'd like to do is aggressive confrontation, but I feel that would be unproductive. On the other hand, simple patience has not worked. I find myself thinking I should try to establish stronger rapport with this woman, helping her to see me as a person. I think I need to visit her one-to-one. I know that simply continuing to analyze the problem just leaves me drained.

Focus Questions

1. Who has the power here and how is it being used?

2. How would you describe the pastor's response to both personal and institutional needs?

3. If ministering to Mrs. Quell's needs does not change the situation, what options should the pastor consider?

20. Cancel The Trip

For half a dozen years, I have served as pastor of Lakeside Lutheran, a congregation of 750 members in a midwestern town of 3,000. The pastor before me had a tenure of 22 years. My style is very different from his. The congregation has journeyed through a multitude of changes, not the least of which is the addition of a secretary and a significant increase in the pastor's salary. As in all congregations, there is grumbling over any change, but most of the congregation has stoically endured or has been favorable to the changes here.

In July, Milford, our Stewardship Chairperson, became angry that my wife and I were attempting to lead a group of members on a trip to Spain. Although the activity had been okayed by the Council, Milford felt it was unethical and dishonest. At a meeting with the Executive Committee of the Council, this activity was discussed, along with others such as visitation, sensitivity to people in a rural community, salary, and help with parsonage repairs. A week later, my wife and I decided that we did not want to offend anyone, so we cancelled the trip to Spain.

This summer my wife and I decided to invest in a part-time vending business which is in her name. She runs it, but I help out whenever my schedule permits.

This all is background to a week-long happening.

Monday night the Executive Committee meets to discuss staff salaries. The salaries of the secretary, janitor, and groundskeeper are dealt with quickly. Because of a $16,000 budget shortfall and an 11-14% increase in healthcare costs, we negotiate a 3.2% raise in my salary. All members of the Executive Committee state that they can support this package.

Wednesday night the Stewardship Committee meets to put the budget together. In the past they have placed salaries proposed by the Executive Committee into the budget without comment.

I arrive late to the meeting due to an earlier appointment. The committee has already dealt with salaries and are into worship and evangelism needs. After one and a half hours, the only thing left is to add up the totals. I begin to excuse myself, but Milford says,

"Pastor, I think you should stay. There are some salary issues which need to be addressed." I take my seat somehow knowing what is coming.

After a short break, the meeting resumes. Milford directs the meeting. "Pastor," he begins, "we have decided that you will not receive an increase in your salary this year."

"Oh," I respond, "I'm surprised at this because it was already decided at the Executive Committee. Am I to pick up some message from this decision to freeze my salary?"

"Yes, I think you can," Milford responds. "We think you should leave."

"What?!"

"I'm shocked," Milford continues, "that you would be so insensitive as to have a vending company in addition to your pastoral duties. It is totally insensitive to the people of this community." Milford was now getting very emotional. "My job demands one hundred percent of my time, and so should yours. There are many people upset and angry at you, Pastor. You are not the pastor they want and need. I've given a great deal of thought to the reasons for our budget shortfall, and I can only conclude that people are not giving because they do not like the way we are spending the budget. They don't like the salary we are paying you. They are not giving, and they are not coming to church."

Two members of the Executive Committee are at the meeting and are silent. One of the other Stewardship Committee members supports Milford and is upset about my other business. The third member of the committee is silent except to say, "I didn't know anything about this."

Thursday my wife and I travel to our synod office and visit with an Assistant to the Bishop. We are given support. We share ideas about resolving the conflict. We are assured we have done nothing wrong.

Saturday afternoon the Executive Committee meets. It is decided that the Stewardship Committee has overstepped its bounds, and the committee is directed to implement the salary increases.

Sunday afternoon the Council meets to adopt the budget. Milford produces budget number one and budget number two. He threatens to resign from the council and leave the congregation if the council adopts the budget containing a salary increase. Milford leaves the meeting. The Council fudges. It adopts the budget but without the increase. Furthermore, it directs the treasurer to open up my salary for discussion during the November semi-annual meeting.

Monday afternoon Milford comes over to talk. He is very emotional. He confesses that he is struggling with other issues in his life. He does not want to continue to carry around the hate he has for me. We talk and basically agree to disagree. During the conversation Milford again stresses that there are people in the congregation who are talking and who are upset.

In response to these unknown people and the inevitable rumors, my wife and I compose a letter explaining what we see as the issues. We include this in the congregation's monthly newsletter.

As I weigh this situation, I realize I have been unsure whether I am dealing with just one person, a small group, or a significant portion of the congregation. The response that I have received from our letter seems to indicate only a small minority.

I believe that much of this boils down to the fact that I am not like my predecessor. In addition, because of his long tenure, I am seen as a stepfather who has "married mom and taken dad's place."

The congregation and I also are struggling with control issues, such as how much my family and I must bend into their image of a pastor and family.

The one thing I would do differently is to have visited Milford on Thursday, the day after the shocking meeting. Perhaps my relationship with him could have been saved. The letter to the congregation was, I believe, a good step. It brought the issues to light. Once that happened, it seems that many of the issues, such as my responsibility for the budget shortfall and worship attendance, have disappeared. Some "alligators" have been identified. I intend to visit them after the annual meeting, not with the thought of resolving issues, but at least keeping up communication with them.

———

Focus Questions

1. Review the several sources for conflict in this situation. How would you weigh those you have identified?

2. Dealing with conflict is like jumping into or maybe being pushed into a rapidly flowing stream; everything is constant motion. What first steps might you recommend this pastor take? Reflect, too, on those he has already taken.

3. How might the pastor's personal ministry to Milford's needs affect this situation? Can he actually do it?

4. If the pastor is right about dealing with "alligators," what shape should his ministry toward them take?

21. Structuring For Mission

Over the years I have been concerned about the bishops of our Lutheran church body "spreading themselves too thin." Congregations and pastors have often felt little oversight from a bishop who tends 200 to 300 congregations over a large geographical area. When bishops or their staff members have arrived on the scene of a congregation, it often has been to put out a "big fire" or celebrate a big event. Little nurturing of healthy day-to-day relationships has taken place, and congregations have been free to be islands unto themselves. A sense of mission beyond the congregation has tended to be limited at best.

For the above reasons and others, when the opportunity for a new Lutheran church body was upon us in the mid-'80s, I began thinking of the possibilities of smaller judicatories for which bishops could exercise oversight. In fact, it was at a meeting of the Academy of Parish Clergy that I was encouraged to write my thoughts and share them with the larger church. This led to an article in our national publication.

In the fall of '85 several pastors affirmed the ideas in that piece and met to explore the possibility of a synod in our Mississippi Valley area of the Midwest where I serve a 1,500-member congregation in a city of 50,000. After several meetings, it was decided to survey the congregations of the area to see if they were interested. A positive response of 65 to 70 percent from church councils encouraged us to ask for congregational votes at 1986 annual meetings. A key element in publicizing this was a color photo and article in our city's daily newspaper serving the area. Again, an endorsement by two thirds of the congregations encouraged us to petition the Commission on the New Lutheran Church (CNLC) to make six rather than five synods in Wisconsin.

Prior to the February 1986 CNLC meeting, the *ad hoc* sixth synod committee called several commission members, especially those working on synod boundaries. The commission approved a sixth synod in Wisconsin pending the advice of the district/synod judicatories at their annual conventions.

The first district to vote approved it by a good majority following vigorous discussion. The second district to vote gave even stronger support. A third judicatory voted against the sixth synod after a strong statement by its bishop.

A Lutheran pastor from that national judicatory within our own city, however, wrote a strong letter to the CNLC prior to its June meeting saying that the overwhelming majority of district/synod people supported the sixth synod. We also called the Wisconsin representatives and the boundary committee to ask for their support. An area man was our chief support on the CNLC, calling us as soon as the vote was taken. He called to say our synod has been approved over the objection of another of our state representatives who viewed the sixth synod addition as evidence of our area's parochialism.

Since the synod received final approval, a team of a dozen from within the new synod boundaries was appointed by the judicatories involved to become our transition team. We have met about ten times to plan and propose a structure for the new synod. It has been an exhilarating experience with every person playing an active role. Currently many more people are being involved in task forces to give detail to our plans. Our synod's constituting convention is to be held to amend and approve our synod's mission.

We who have worked in this movement have felt that it has strengthened our sense of mission in the new Lutheran body. We believe congregations will have better oversight from our synod bishop and will be better connected to the world mission of the church.

———

Focus Questions

1. From the information above, what do you consider the key factors, including pastoral ones, in the successful formation of this new synod?

2. On what grounds would you argue whether the decision to form a new synod was either a) evidence of parochialism or b) service for the church's mission?

3. How would you determine several years later the wisdom or success of this synod's formation?

22. Deciding To Relocate

A few individuals at Community Church, a Methodist congregation of 250 adults in a midwestern town, have discussed the possibility of constructing a new church building for at least four or five years. The present church is landlocked on a main street corner by streets and a school. Some people have been expressing the concern that the process to consider building has been taking far too long. When I was assigned to this church two and one-half years ago, I was asked by my superintendent to help bring this discussion to a successful conclusion for the congregation. Using our denomination structure, I dissolved an established committee set up for long-range planning and formed a new committee with new personnel. The intention was to achieve the end of having the whole congregation, not just an "in" crowd, make the decision.

The newly established committee worked for a full year. Members spoke with contractors within the community on various options. They spoke about how best to improve the existing facility with handicap ramps, elevators, second floors, basements, and purchase of additional land — to name the most obvious options. Community Church, by the way, has neither a parking lot nor existing adjacent property. The committee also researched the possibility of a new facility on what is projected to be the growing edge of town in the future. This whole process was painstakingly long for those who were already anxious to build.

The committee voted by secret ballot on which project to endorse to the full membership. The committee split ten to three in favor of the building choice. Now the congregation had to be approached for its decision. On the four Sundays prior to the annual meeting, a speaker from the committee presented his or her opinion and personal feelings on the current situation. Four people were chosen by the chair for this, two persons he felt were in favor of building, and two who had expressed their doubts.

The proposal was presented at the annual congregational meeting. At this time a report of both sets of findings, remodel or build, was shared with the membership, with the recommendation to build a new structure. Ordinarily, fifteen to thirty members have appeared at this congregation's annual meeting, but this time 53 members were present for the decision. The result? Moving forward on the new building route by a vote of 43 to 10.

Decisions like this can rend a congregation wide open. One real challenge is enabling a process which allows the congregation to dream and plan for the future without losing people in the rush forward. On the other side, too much time may elapse. Either extreme is undesirable. I have some new insights to how Christ might have felt working with his disciples, some wishing to die fighting, others cowering in the face of the authorities.

To this point I feel I have walked through the process with a fair amount of deftness. By very carefully involving a cross section of the congregation, nearly all perspectives of Community Church were able to be voiced and respected. In the church family I think I was able to allow Christian fellowship to be offered to both supporters and dissenters. We have not lost members over the matter, although some of the most enthusiastic supporters — who anticipated this outcome — have pulled back with frustration at what they feel to be the sluggishness of the project's progress. They too need to feel respected and will need to be kept included in the congregation's vision for the future.

———

Focus Questions

1. How would you characterize the role of the pastor in this process?

2. Process is described as key in this case, which appears successful. Are there any missing elements?

3. If you were the pastor, what obvious obstacles or hidden land mines should you be alert to as the process continues?

23. What About Our Future?

Button Hole Methodist Church is a very old rural Wisconsin congregation of 85 adults and is set in the open country. Button Hole is not a community but a geographical place known throughout the area. The congregation will be celebrating its one hundred twentieth anniversary next year. It has 85 members, 83 percent of them blood relation. At one time the congregation had a membership roster of some 120 members, but the numbers have fallen off for two reasons. First, the young people are moving to other places after they have gone off to college; second, the farm economy has forced many of the small old farms to close. Where there once were ten farms on the Button Hole Road, for instance, there now are three. The worshiping community has become mostly retired farmers and their spouses. About thirty persons attend worship each Sunday. The Sunday School program includes about eleven children and ten adults. Only eight of Button Hole's members live away from the community.

The Button Hole Administrative Council met for its monthly meeting. At this time we learned that the treasurer had $408 in the checking account. There is, as I recall, also $750 in an Improvement Fund and another $200 in a Memorial Fund. The treasurer reported that she has not paid any more than two thirds of one month's apportionments for the year, even though we are now halfway through the year. This information prompted a discussion about "how nobody cares about our church." This is not a new topic. The frustration over finances soon moved into frustration over the lack of interest from young people.

I have noticed that there is a key group at Button Hole called the Founders who have been strong throughout the history of the congregation. A large share of the group is now composed of couples in their late fifties and early sixties. They also constitute the main body who attend worship, teach Sunday School, and hold Administrative Council office. As a result, almost all irritation is expressed toward the non-Founders. It may also be important to note that nearly all congregational events are a result of Founders' plans.

There has come to be a stalemate in any discussion about mission. The talk about giving always turns toward the depressing level of involvement, the farm economy, or sons and daughters departing the community. The whole situation tends to become depressing and frustrating.

In the past two years I have seen the congregation pay $10,000 for a new septic system, side the sanctuary for another $10,000, and rebuild the basement interior for $7,000. These are in addition to the congregation's paying its apportionments for the first time in eight years. I believe these programs have successfully called for ownership by the whole congregation. At the same time, these needs did result in some increase in regular support, but only some, because regular operations are interpreted as the plans of the Founders and not the whole congregation.

I believe two things are true here. First, the greater the need, the stronger the support; and second, the more people involved, the more ownership they will take. I have heard it said that if the whole is not involved, those excluded will attempt to undermine the program.

I am planning to meet with the persons outside the Founders to get their feelings about the church. Special programs may be fine, but they do not serve to deepen spiritual faith. A deliberate mission program can provide a longer lasting ownership and involvement in the life of Button Hole. I want to talk with these persons about these possibilities and their need and so increase their bodily involvement at church. I feel that my listening and talking to them will tell these people that the congregation and I as their pastor care about their involvement. At the same time as I try to involve non-Founders in the planning of Button Hole's future, it is important for me to tend to the needs and the egos of the Founders.

I feel torn between being totally responsible for the future of Button Hole Church and knowing that Button Hole's members hold future success or failure in their hands with me facilitating communication. I am prepared to be caught in a crossfire. It is very possible that the Founders will feel that they are losing power in the congregation as they approach their retirement years. They are not the only ones who can feel threatened, however, but also those

who take the reins and become responsible for the successes and
failures down the road.

_____

Focus Questions

1. In terms of power issues, how would you describe Button
Hole's situation? What do think of the pastor's analysis?

2. What are the needs, perceived and actual, of this congregation? What are the power issues?

3. The pastor speaks of being prepared to be caught in a
crossfire. What are his alternatives, either avoiding such a situation or if he does get caught in it?

4. What are theological and spiritual resources this pastor and
congregation can draw upon?

24. The Girl At The Grave

As Methodist pastor of a 300-member congregation in a small midwestern city, I was called by the funeral home director to minister to an unchurched family. I had no previous contact with the family. They live in a community 28 miles away. I was called because someone in the deceased's family had a Methodist background. The deceased himself, Mr. Tollick, was seventy years old and not active in any congregation. When I arrived at the funeral home, I learned the family was three adults and two children. One was Mr. Tollick's ex-wife, who appeared to be in her early thirties, but the other relationships were unclear to me. I was told he had a fifteen-year-old daughter, but that her whereabouts were unknown. As I walked into the chapel to begin the service, the funeral director said something in passing about Mr. Tollick's having "done time" but I knew nothing more. Following the service, I felt led to make myself available to the people gathered when Mr. Tollick's ashes were returned for interment.

When the ashes were returned, I went to the cemetery with the funeral director. As we arrived, I saw two women from the funeral talking with a teenage girl dressed in black "biker style" clothing. I thought this odd attire for a hot August afternoon. I presumed this might be the daughter and I was right. I spoke to the three women gathered there, seeking to offer words of comfort. Then we held the committal service, and I remained with those gathered. I spoke to the girl, sensing within her feelings of being distanced. As we talked, the mother of Miss Tollick revealed that she had been sexually molested by her father, the deceased. That was the reason the girl had been absent earlier, the woman explained, and why she and Tollick had divorced. I made a mental note that this probably explained the earlier reference to "doing time."

The mother clearly wanted her daughter to talk, and much to my surprise, Miss Tollick felt comfortable enough to speak with me. I anticipated anger, but instead, she expressed concern about her father being forgiven by God. She knew what he had done was wrong, but she said she also had good memories and did not want to think of him spending eternity in hell. I wondered to myself if

83

she were experiencing an unresolved guilt. Aloud I assured her that God would be fair, and I worked into my conversation my belief that what had happened was not her fault. She was the victim of a man who was sick. This seemed accepted as we talked.

Miss Tollick needed forgiveness. She carried with her a great deal of anger, which was reflected in her dramatic attire. I knew there was something more to this story, but what it was, I was not sure. My openness to her allowed her to reveal what was on her mind. I had hoped I was not rushing her to deal with something too quickly, but I knew my time and opportunity here would be very limited, so why not try the best God could give me to do?

I believe I did the right thing. I was deeply appreciative of my training, my faith, and my willingness to "trust my gut." I had sensed something did not feel right when I first met this family, but it required some time and energy to begin to unravel the mystery. It was well worth it. My regret is that this family is so disjointed and I myself have no way of following up on them. I hope and trust that I was able to bring some sense or possibility of forgiveness into the situation. Guilt and shame are heavy burdens to bear, let alone having to face your future carrying them. I believe Miss Tollick needed that assurance of forgiveness.

Instead of the biblical woman at the well, I met the girl at the grave. The parallel seemed significant. I wanted to offer her the sunshine of life so that she might be able to shed the black cloud hanging over her heart. The black leather jacket, jeans, and boots are deeply etched into my memory. The glint of sunshine reflected on the buckles was merely a hint of what needed to be unbound emotionally and spiritually. I wonder how free she feels. For myself, I am aware that even brief moments of ministry require high energy.

Focus Questions

1. Given this description, how would you describe the need in the situation?

84

2. How would you describe the limits and possibilities within the pastor's role here?

3. Is this ministry opportunity concluded? Why or why not?

25. Am I Worth Anything?

Eunice is a 32-year-old woman with one child from her first marriage. A woman of normal height and weight, she presents herself as attractive and self-assured, although inwardly she was not the latter. She came to me, her Disciples of Christ pastor, with a need, as she said, "To see myself in a different way, to learn to value myself." I serve her congregation of 200 families in a midwestern town.

Her diagnosis on the DSM-III is that of a depressed, borderline personality disorder. Her somatic symptoms include intermittent migraines and chest pains. Her stressors have diminished over the last few years, but she is unsatisfied with her general feelings of not being able to cope. She says she feels she is "on the edge of not functioning."

She is the younger daughter with a younger brother and an older sister, all siblings of an alcoholic father and a passive-dependent mother. An older brother died in infancy. She feels that her father leaned on her older sister and she herself could never win her father's affection. She felt close to her mother, but her mother did nothing to help the relationship between her and her father. Thus, she felt that women were weak and she was unable to win approval from anyone — unless she earned it by being especially good or helpful. Consequently, she grew up as the rescuer in several relationships. A complicating factor was her lack of trusting men due not only to her father's cool relationship toward her, but also due to a male relative who fondled her breasts when she was entering puberty. She remembers her drunken father pushing her mother against the wall with a shotgun. Her frustrations and feelings of valuelessness led her to a failed suicide attempt before she came to see me.

In her psycho-sexual history she said she married to get out of the house. Understandably, she married her surrogate father, an alcoholic who would not hold a job and who beat her. She had a daughter by him but divorced him after some five years of abuse. This was a positive effort on her part to move beyond her mother's

86

passivity and her own low self-valuing. These were points helpful to her for increasing her assertiveness and growing self-valuing.

Eunice was able to develop a relationship with a single man in our church whom she married. Her earlier marital rejection by her alcoholic husband and her feelings of paternal rejection led her to project such feelings upon her second husband that she felt he also was rejecting her. Intellectually she knew that he loved her, but emotionally she had terrible difficulty accepting his love.

In my work with her, I first had her sign a "Contract for Living." My therapy focused on her development of self-valuing feelings. A Gestalt two-chair exercise helped her finally terminate the molesting male relative's influence on her. Reality checks helped her learn to see her second husband's behavior in a positive light so that she could accept him. Therapy helped her deal with clients whom she regarded as discounting her when they did such things as fail to meet their schedules. Structural and transactional therapy assisted her to view her parents' attitude toward her in realistic ways. She admitted that since she is now a "grown-up woman and not a little girl back home," she can talk straight with her parents for the first time in her life. Eunice and her husband at this time are happily married and very active in our congregation.

Focus Questions

1. How would you describe the need of this woman?

2. Her pastor obviously has significant psychological tools at hand. Assuming you did not have those same tools, how would you diagnose her and respond?

3. For example, specifically what resources could be drawn upon to move this from intellectually knowing about love to experientially feeling it?

4. What biblical or theological resources might a person bring to bear?

5. What is the healing role for the congregation in Eunice's life?

26. I Could Be Sued

These were not ordinary days for me. I pastor a 400-member Methodist congregation in a midwestern town of 4,000. Last week I spent parts of two days in Circuit Court with Dan and Marlene Karras, two longtime active members of our congregation. Dan and his brother Ben operate an insurance agency which does a good deal of business insuring farmers against property loss and liability claims. They were being sued by a farm partnership who claimed that the Karrases had misrepresented the policy they had sold the farmers. The farmers had learned, following a particular type of accident they had caused, that it was not in fact covered by the policy.

After my time in court, I ended up feeling that the Karrases had established far better credibility than had the farmers; nevertheless, the jury found the Karrases to have misrepresented the policy to the detriment of the farm partnership. A dollar judgment has not yet been determined.

My involvement was primarily that of moral support for the Karrases. That experience, however, has led me to do some reflecting on the issue of clergy malpractice.

How critical is malpractice insurance for pastors, and for me, in particular? To give this some grounding, let me reflect on a situation from a previous congregation I served.

Mike and Debbie were going through a divorce. They had an eight-year-old daughter, Susan. Mike had been diagnosed as a schizophrenic and, according to Debbie, had threatened both her and Susan with a knife. From my dealings with the family, I concluded that Debbie had her own problems with paranoia, that Mike was little, if any, threat to his daughter, and that it was in Susan's best interest (and Mike's legal right) that she maintain contact with her father. I wrote a letter to the Family Court Commissioners to that effect.

My reflections on this situation lead me to ask several questions. What if Mike is granted visitation rights over Debbie's objections, and furthermore, what if he were in fact to harm Susan? Could Debbie have sued me for malpractice?

89

The saying is: "You can always sue; the question is, can you prevail?" That statement, however, does not account for another reality. Any suit, founded or not, needs to be defended. And that can be expensive.

On the other hand, ministry is a calling of risk. We could ask: Aren't we spiritually desensitizing ourselves when we build a legal wall around our vulnerability? Furthermore, what message does this convey to the world? It is a known fact that very possession of insurance is in itself an invitation to be sued.

My actual situation is that I carry malpractice insurance as a rider on our congregation's policy. Ironically enough, we are serviced by the Karras agency. I asked that the congregation add this insurance, not because I think my practice is incompetent, but because, like all clergy, I work occasionally with unstable people and I don't want to risk a suit which might sacrifice my children's access to higher education.

————

Focus Questions

1. Consider the appropriateness of the pastor's involvement in the two situations he describes, especially given the possible legal issues.

2. The pastor calls ministry "a calling of risk." Is that so? If it is, then what might be called appropriate risk?

3. To what extent might the threat of a suit impact the doing of ministry?

27. Those Hymns You Choose!

Mrs. Orinski is the wife of a retired former Lutheran senior pastor of our 2,000-member congregation located in a Plains state town of 10,000. She and her husband returned here four years ago after spending several retirement years as members of a church in another state where, she said emphatically, "The pastor did not make us feel at all welcome."

Since arriving here Mrs. Orinski has become the regular Bible study leader of her women's small group, has held office in the umbrella women's group in our congregation, and currently presides over the retirees' organization in the congregation. Her husband has taught classes and preached here on several occasions. In spite of these involvements and the respect which goes with them, she frequently has been critical of us who are the congregation's pastors and sometimes of the congregational direction. She also keeps reminding us that her husband is "the only pastor emeritus of the congregation" and deserves special recognition.

At 9:00 a.m. one weekday morning, Mrs. Orinski stopped by my office without appointment on her way to work with another committee. She asked me what I had meant by something I had said to her at a Bible study leaders' meeting three weeks previous, namely, that I had said she was "very opinionated" when we had been discussing the hymns our congregation sings at worship. I reminded her of the context in which the discussion had taken place, how group members were asked to respond to "ways our congregation reaches out to others," and how she had introduced her unhappiness with hymn choices at that point and several points following. After several efforts to move the discussion back on track, I had used those words and had intended, I now added, that she held strong opinions and was most persistent in them. She then indicated that she had been deeply hurt by my words and that several women present could not understand my saying that to her. I apologized for saying these words which hurt her, confessing that they had probably come out of my own frustration to get back to what I perceived to be the task at hand. I emphasized again that my intent was not to hurt her, and I was sorry for the pain she had been caused.

I sensed that she heard my apology. Then she proceeded to tell me again that our selection of hymns and how they were played deeply troubled her. In fact, she said, this music was driving older people away from the church. (I chose not to challenge her on this last unsubstantiated statement.) She said she made a point of not voicing her unhappiness to others, but she wanted me to know how greatly troubled she was for the church. I responded that I sincerely appreciated her concern and that we pastors continued to use as our rule of thumb that we have no more than one new hymn per Sunday. At the same time, I added, the diversity in our congregation is so great on this subject that she and I would probably never see eye-to-eye on it. She also informed me that she had volunteered, when they first returned, to help organize evangelism efforts in the congregation but that I had never asked her. I had to admit to her I had no recollection of this. Shortly, she excused herself to attend her committee meeting.

Mrs. Orinski obviously had been brooding over my words and needed to share her hurt feelings. It seems that her encounter with me is part and parcel of a continuing need to receive affirmation and recognition of her personal worth. My words, spoken ("opinionated") and unspoken (not asking her to help with evangelism), were perceived by her as put-downs. At the same time, she not only seems to need to express her opinions, but also to gain acceptance of them in order to feel satisfied.

At the time I told Mrs. Orinski that I felt she was "very opinionated," I remember being frustrated and inwardly angry at her persistence and her inconsideration of our purpose in meeting together. I think it was right and necessary that I apologize. At the same time, while I do not regret dealing strongly with her at that initial meeting, I could have chosen better words and perhaps set up a special time to take up her subject. I could not, in any case, "solve" her problem. I could describe present practice and policy, which I did, letting her know that the pastoral staff struggles with a diversity of congregational opinion. How she is affirmed and how she exercises her influence in our congregation continue to be matters of real concern, matters perhaps eased but hardly solved by her occupying positions of power.

––––––––

Focus Questions

1. How would you define "the problem" in this case?

2. Was the pastor correct in believing that he should apologize, or was this a dangerous concession?

3. What does Mrs. Orinski need?

4. What would constitute a good ministry to Mrs. Orinski? After all, she is now one of the members of this congregation.

28. Faded Dreams

He was one mad farmer! You see, he and his neighbor had shared equipment and time at haying and harvesting for the past several years. This morning he had watched the neighbor pull a load of hay toward the barn only to notice one wheel on the wagon wasn't turning. The wagon was pulled like a mud sled by the powerful tractor as smoke curled from the dragged tire. Now the farmer was in town buying parts and unfreezing the wheel from the axle. This is in a midwestern town where I serve as the Disciples of Christ pastor to 200 families.

I walked up as he was telling the mechanic what had happened. After listening for a moment, I asked, "By the way, where is Steve?" "Oh, he's over there (he jerked his thumb toward the local beer hall) getting lubricated. If he had lubricated this wheel one percent as much as himself we'd have every wheel on the farm spinning."

Sensing his frustration and helpless anger, I said little and watched the men work on the wheel. A recent memory formed in my mind as I recalled Steve's wife phoning me one morning for a talk about his drinking. Although I left for their place immediately, Steve was already on the way to the hayfield. He didn't want to talk with her pastor. For an hour his wife poured out her frustration, anger, hopelessness, and despair over the broken dreams of her marriage and home.

She had never dated anyone but him. He had seemed so amiable and fun to be with. He was from a respected Catholic home; she had faithfully attended a rural United Methodist Church. There should be no trouble with religious differences, she thought. In part, she was right: he never attended any church, Catholic or other. Gradually, her own faith seemed no match for his drinking and consequent behavior. What was worse, she said, was her loss of respect and love for him.

He was the younger of two sons. His dad once told me that his dream was to leave each son a thousand acres of land and a few hundred cattle. He had almost realized his goal by the time the older son phoned one morning to tell me, "Dad passed away a

94

while ago ... out feeding the stock ... heart attack, I guess." I went right over.

It is strange how memories flood one's soul from simple events such as a frozen wheel. My memories continued as I thanked God that out here in the country one did not question religious affiliation. One simply met the pain of life's crises and crosses. One supported and helped the suffering to know that God loves us and cares infinitely. So the son and his family and I talked about the father, how he had cared for his family, how he had dreamed for his two boys, how the responsibility for the farm would now be shared between the two who were left. Tears from the grief, smiles of happy incidents, precious shared experiences mingled as we talked. The Holy Spirit comforted each one while we held hands and prayed our thanks for this father who loved his family and neighbors. We thanked God for our hope of life beyond death through the resurrection of Jesus Christ. The prayer ended, and our hands unclasped. I remembered the quiet calm as tears were unabashedly wiped away and some smiles of trust smoothed the sorrowing faces.

Suddenly my reverie of remembrance was interrupted by the mechanic saying, "Well, it's finally unstuck." I thought that was a timely remark not only for the wheel, but for the family who had found a way to get unstuck from their saddest time. Then my mind abruptly returned to the morning conversation with Steve's wife. "What hurts and scares me, Pastor, is that Steve is a stranger in our house. The kids don't know when their dad is going to be interested in them or yell at them." We talked of her heartbreak at unrealized expectations in marriage; we spoke of her unrequited efforts to make a go of it. She admitted her panic at seeing her home broken in spite of anything she could do. She felt she had failed her parents, her children, herself, everyone, by failing in her marriage. "Have you failed?" I asked. "It seems to me it takes two to make a marriage. If one refuses, in spite of everything, to be married...." My voice trailed off as I noticed her eyes seemed to have moved on.

What she momentarily was thinking she dimly revealed. "I could divorce him, but, if I go on...." And she stopped. I had heard her "if" and I quietly said, "Do you want to tell me what you were thinking?" After a few moments when tears washed down her cheeks, she confessed, "I could just do away with myself!" Her anguish had its nearly final outburst. We talked about her value to herself and her children, to me and her church. I saw an old envelope on the table and hastily wrote, "I will not in any way do myself, or anyone else, any harm to the body or mind. When I feel down, I will get in touch with Pastor (*name*), or someone whom I can trust, and talk. I sign this Contract for Living, God helping me." "Nancy," I said, "will you read and sign this contract? I'll sign under your name. Keep this where you know it is and read it often." She signed it. Eventually she confronted him, and they both decided to talk with me. We moved into a series of counseling sessions, and I rejoiced the day they and their children came together to church. The wheel finally is fixed — and so is this family. Both will need care, however, for as long as life endures.

Focus Questions

1. The pastor successfully used a Contract for Living with the wife, who was the immediate concern. What other options or resources would a pastor have for helping her?

2. All the problems seem to center around the drinking. Is there any way the pastor might have dealt more assertively with this, especially if the wife had not confronted her husband?

3. What kind of continuing care may be needed for this family?

29. Finding Support

Smithville is a community of 1,500 located about sixty miles from the center of a metropolitan area in the Midwest. Due to this proximity, Smithville has been experiencing rapid change from a mostly rural town to a "bedroom" community. This has resulted in challenges for the business community, the economic base of the community and, predictably, the "family" dynamics of a once rural town.

The Smithville Christian community is served by five congregations: ELCA Lutheran, Roman Catholic, Lutheran Church-Missouri Synod, American Baptist, and Mission Covenant. Average worship attendances for each are 270, 180, 120, 80, and 50, respectively. The clergy leaders of these congregations all arrived within the past four years. Among them, the ELCA pastor, Tomson, the American Baptist pastor, Jack, and the Roman Catholic priest, Royce, are the most active in the local clergy association. The group was meeting in "boast and brag" and "moan and groan" sessions with a focus on planning shared leadership in community ecumenical functions.

Due to the nature of community change, each of the congregations in the community began to experience some conflicts. While much of the conflict was directed toward clergy, the real issues seemed to have to do with power struggles between the "newcomers" and "old-timers," the nature of pastoral leadership, the transfer of leadership, and decision-making dynamics. The clergy involved were largely unaware of the experiences of their colleagues.

Beginning Palm Sunday and culminating on Maundy Thursday, Father Royce received the resignation of his entire leadership team, which consisted of two paid staff and the parish council. The resignations were largely unexpected and indirect, for example, leaving messages on the answering machine or under the office door while Father Royce was saying Mass. This experience was so traumatic that he called Pastors Tomson and Jack on Good Friday afternoon for support and prayer.

As Father Royce shared his experiences, Pastors Tomson and Jack heard a story which also was largely their own, with some variations. The three clergy agreed to meet prayerfully, vulnerably, and supportively during Easter week to share stories and offer support. The sharing session lasted more than three hours. During it the clergy discovered that each was experiencing similar dynamics in his personal life, his ministry, and his congregation. They came to understand that what appeared to be a "just me" experience was in fact the experience of their colleagues. This discovery revealed a much broader community problem and issue.

With this beginning, these three clergy covenanted to attend a workshop together, to meet weekly for prayer and support, and to keep in touch with each other for insights into community dynamics. Trust was of such a level that individual situations were openly discussed among them. They attend a seminar on "Co-dependent Organizations" at which they learned many insights into the community, their congregations, and themselves.

The final result of this sharing was the collaboration of the three for a series of sermons preached during Lent. The three clergy cooperatively agreed on the scripture readings, wrote the sermons, and announced that the same series of sermons was being preached in all three congregations. The sermons and their content became a regular topic of conversation at local gatherings.

The ability of these clergy to move beyond "moaning and groaning" enabled them to continue in effective ministry in the community. Pastor Tomson and Father Royce stayed for at least eight more years, and Pastor Jack for two more until his judicatory minister negotiated a termination of this call. Equally important, these clergy did not burn out. They neither succumbed to their congregations' pressures for immediate resignations, nor did they regress into their own destructive behavior patterns.

Focus Questions

1. In this case what do you see as the most constructive behaviors?

2. What might have happened had the clergy not shared their experiences with each other?

3. What made it possible for these clergy to be vulnerable to each other? Is the same possible in your own clergy association? Elaborate.

4. Short of a crisis, how can clergy begin to move beyond "brag and boast" or "moan and groan" gatherings?

30. The Eavesdropper

My 1,500-member Lutheran congregation is situated in a Plains state town of 7,000. Mrs. Waters has been our custodian for seven years. Her husband does much of the heavy custodial work for us in a half-time capacity. Prior to her assuming this position, Mrs. Waters served as a cleaning woman for a substantial number of local households. Mrs. Waters is one of those persons living in a small town who delights in making everyone else's business her own. There is nothing which seems to give her greater pleasure whenever the church staff assembles, formally or in informal coffee gatherings, than for her to share some tidbit gleaned from the community just moments earlier. If she cannot relate an incident first, she might be heard to say, "Well, that's just what I was going to say...." She makes that statement so many times a day, even after someone has shared material which she in no way could ever have known!

The issue is this. Our church's phone system is not all that complicated. We have lines coming into the secretary's office and the pastors' offices. There are two phones in other parts of the building with access to the same lines. One of these is in a large community room where Mrs. Waters often has a large amount of cleaning to do. For some time now, the secretaries in the office were noticing on incoming calls that there was either a rather hollow sound or the click of another receiver being lifted. They could not be absolutely sure, they told me, but these two phenomena seemed always to occur when Mrs. Waters was on duty. The secretaries were most concerned that Mrs. Waters was listening in on the conversations. This bothered them significantly, since many calls were of a confidential nature. They also were well aware of the fact that the conversational material shared by folks calling in and heard by Mrs. Waters would soon become the next hot news in town.

The secretaries brought this problem to my attention. I knew that the clamps had to be applied, but in such a way that our custodian would not get terribly defensive and feel totally "found out." I felt that the way to approach this problem was through a discussion of phone protocol at a regularly scheduled meeting of our full congregation staff. We discussed the fact that the secretaries were the ones to answer all incoming calls, including those coming in on the pastors' private line, that others could answer when the secretaries were not present, and finally that the nature of the many incoming calls was confidential and always must be respected as such. This is our obligation to the congregation and one another, we affirmed.

By sharing this information with the entire staff, I felt that it would not be intimidating for Mrs. Waters, but I also felt confident that she would get the drift. If all could hear the message, it also would get full coverage and the entire staff would be reminded of our legitimate concerns for confidentiality and, simply, for good manners.

Mrs. Waters has a rather fragile personality. She reacts rather emotionally to any kind of confrontation. I feel it is better for the sake of good staff relations to keep a positive sense of trust among us all, but at the same time, if there are issues or concerns to be addressed, to share them with the entire staff. Everyone then has the same information and can act upon it, including, if necessary, by changing one's ways. Mrs. Waters has changed her behavior and we have not had further problems in this area.

––––––––––

Focus Questions

1. Given the fact that Mrs. Waters was only suspected of breaking confidentiality, not actually witnessed, are there other appropriate options for handling this situation?

2. Discuss the relevance of Mrs. Waters' personality to the way the situation was handled.

3. Did this achieve the pastor's desire to keep trust within the staff?

31. People's Court

Bob and Dave, both in their late twenties, have been members of American Baptist Church all their short lives, albeit inactively these last few years. Both sets of parents have been active and involved for years. Additionally, Bob's mother is Christian Education and Music Director at our Great Lakes state congregation in this city of 40,000. We have about 300 worshipers each Sunday.

Dave discovered that Bob was having an extramarital affair with his wife. As a result of this knowledge, Dave physically assaulted Bob on two separate occasions. Dave was arrested and charged with attempted murder.

At the request of Dave and his parents, I attended his preliminary hearing. One week after the hearing, Bob's parents confronted me and asked that I "back off" from the case. It was their feeling that it was inappropriate for me to be involved. I assured them that I stood ready to support both them and Dave's family during this difficult time. My problem was that only one family seemed to want my support.

At the request of Dave and his family, I attended a second hearing. After I returned from court that day, I was confronted by Bob's parents. His mother — she's on our staff, remember — was outraged that I went to court "in spite of their request that I remove myself from involvement." A discussion followed in which I attempted to understand why she was so against my lending support to this family in crisis. Our discussion did not resolve the matter and it ended with both of us standing firm in our positions.

I can appreciate that Bob's parents might harbor ill feelings for the way their son has been treated by Dave. Bob continues to live with the fear that Dave might come after him again and cause him additional harm. I do not understand the reasons that Bob and his parents have for rejecting my attempts to lend support to them during this crisis. Furthermore, I resent the fact that they have insisted that I refuse the calls for support that Dave and his family have asked from me as their pastor.

It would be easy for me to support both these families without taking sides. The fact that Bob's family refuses support while

Dave's family welcomes it only makes it more difficult for me. I feel that my decision to support Dave and his family through all of this was the right thing to do. The fact that Bob's family disagrees with me and that his mother is on my staff makes it more difficult. Perhaps there were other options I did not consider.

Focus Questions

1. Consider the pastor's question: were there other options the pastor might have considered earlier when the matters of supporting both families came up?

2. What pastoral matters and spiritual needs of people remain unaddressed in the written form of this case? Could these have a bearing on the matter of accepting pastoral care?

3. Consider whether it is a realistic situation to be pastor for both the accused and the victim. Are there reasons besides one family's refusal why that seems to have failed here?

32. Why Aren't They Here?

Where were they? It was the second Sunday in a row that, unannounced, our volunteer choir director, Pat Taylor, and her husband, Ross, were absent from worship. Pat, about forty years old, is an active member of our 150-member rural-suburban congregation in an eastern state. She could be counted on to lead choir practice before church. Her husband of a similar age sang in our choir of young and middle-aged adults. Pat and Ross have three children. Their absences occurred around Ash Wednesday, and no one at church seemed to know why they were missing. It wasn't like them to miss without giving some notice they would be away.

As their pastor for the past few years, I decided to call the Taylors to find out what was the matter and to be of any help if I could. I began by calling Pat at her work place, since that was where I would most likely reach her. I had suspected that there was trouble in their marriage from clues I had noticed at church. Ross, always casually dressed, frequently jokes around and enjoys making sexual double entendres. He openly flirted with another congregational member who seemed to like his juvenile attentions. On one occasion, Ross mercilessly teased Pat about a recipe she'd prepared which had ended in disaster. Pat did not respond in kind. She comes to church well-dressed and prepared for leading the choir, something she obviously enjoys. She has a sense of humor but is not flippant like her husband. I find her to be an intelligent and caring person.

When I first called Pat, I expressed my concern and interest in her and Ross, and I waited for a response. She began to weep and sob, barely getting out any words. Finally, she blurted, "I want to tell you soon what is wrong, but I can't do it yet." I assured her of our love and prayers and then asked her to give me a call and set up a meeting date very soon. A day or two later she called and we met that afternoon in my office after she got off work. Pat said that Ross had packed his bags and left home. She did not know where he was or why he was gone. She had met with a marriage counselor and, after getting a phone call from Ross, made an appointment for them to see the counselor together. I assured her that, of course, this news would be kept in confidence. She asked me to tell the choir members who had asked about them that she would be back to church soon. She was reluctant to attend church in the meantime since questions would be asked and she wasn't ready to answer anyone yet. I then suggested that she come to her Sunday School class. There she could find peers whose friendship, love, support, and prayer would help carry her through this crisis in her marriage. She did this and it was very helpful. There were a lot of tears and hugs the day she came to her class. I met with her once more in my office for counseling.

As is sometimes the case, Ross had left Pat for another woman with whom he is now living. Pat was enraged at this. She exclaimed, "My husband is either a coward or an idiot!" I tried to help Pat vent her anger and think some thoughts aloud. She and her husband had been to a marriage counselor, but he had been very reticent to share anything at all unless asked specifically. He refused to keep further appointments. He left his line of work and found another job.

A timely phone call, a listening ear, a helpful suggestion, prayers, a marriage counselor, the support of work friends and church friends, and her children and I helped Pat begin to weather the crisis in her marriage and life.

––––––

Focus Questions

1. Consider the clues provided here that a marriage was in trouble and their importance to doing ministry.

2. The pastor appeared to intervene assertively and effectively. What are strengths in his approach? What might have been additional options?

3. The pastor is pastor to both Pat and her husband Ross. What were or are the possibilities of ministry to him?

33. An Added Bit Of Persuasion

The trustees meeting had been rather uneventful until that moment when Alice, an active 69-year-old "pillar of the church," said, "I'd like to know who authorized putting that bulletin board in the narthex, and why?" This was taking place in a Methodist congregation of 400 adults in a midwestern city of 60,000 people.

Although the question caught me totally by surprise, I did, in fact, know the answer. I explained as calmly as possible that it had been authorized by the Administrative Board in response to a concern which came out of a retreat some months earlier for better internal communications within the congregation. Alice insisted that, for aesthetic reasons, the bulletin board should be taken down and the decision of the Board reversed. After an embarrassingly long silence, the chair of the trustees agreed to take the matter to the next Board meeting. The discussion from the Administrative Board meeting essentially amounted to this, "It's too bad someone is offended, but the bulletin board stays."

A couple weeks later at the fall bazaar, Alice made some comments within the hearing of the church secretary about the quality of the display the latter had put on the board. These comments distinctly upset the church secretary. Our annual pledge campaign was conducted a couple weeks later, and Alice's response came back, "I am holding my pledge in abeyance until such time as the bulletin board is removed."

I decided it was time to visit Alice. I had three goals: 1) not further antagonizing her, 2) trying to discern if I were missing something, and 3) allowing her to express herself on what I assessed was fundamentally a power issue. I dropped by unannounced one afternoon. I was welcomed into her home and the ensuing conversation was more matter-of-fact than warm. In response to my offering her my understanding, "It must be difficult sometimes to see some of the younger folks taking over," she responded, "Now, wait a minute. You sound like I am the only one who feels this way; there are others." We parted friends, but no closer to agreeing on the issue than when we had begun.

Our next encounter was at the following trustees meeting when she again attacked the display as being of a level that a "first or second grade class could put up." I said, "Alice, I want you to know that I put that bulletin board display up, and I am personally offended that you should consider my artistic ability to be that of a six- or seven-year-old." She responded, "Well, I am sorry you feel that way about it, but that's what I feel." She then mentioned her withholding of her pledge, and said, "If that bulletin board is worth $980 to the church, so be it." After a little more silence, the chair moved us to the next item.

So far as I know, the last mention of the issue was a 45-minute conversation Alice had with our Lay Assistant, an assertive young woman who gave not an inch. That was two months ago.

In reflecting on this, I am aware that Alice was on the planning committee when the present building was constructed. I have since learned that this is not the first time in the ensuing thirty years that she has reacted this way. I do believe she has an honest concern about preserving the aesthetic integrity of the building. In fact, that may be as far as the issue goes, for as nearly as I can determine, she did practically nothing to marshall support for her position.

I have mixed feelings about the outcome. On the positive side, I feel I handled the conflict well, minimizing the damage in a situation which had no potential for resolution. My statement at the trustees meeting was intentional, designed to publicly call her to accountability for the pain caused by her pot shots at the staff. I have felt throughout that I have been on top of the situation.

On the other hand, I now am finding that I really have a difficult time being nice to Alice. My anger level is pretty high, and I am fearful that someday something might trigger me to act in an inappropriate manner. I also think that I am carrying guilt over feeling that I really don't care to function as her pastor any more.

Focus Questions

1. Consider the strengths and weaknesses of this pastor's management of this conflict situation.

2. Sometimes the welfare of the organization and that of the individual seem, or in fact are, at odds. On what basis does it appear this pastor based his decisions, and what do you think of that?

3. What kind of ministry does Alice need from this congregation and pastor?

4. What kind of spiritual growth could come to the pastor out of this? How might that happen?

34. A Time To Die

I have been taking pastoral care of a family for almost twenty years in the Lutheran 250-member congregation I serve in a town of 19,000 in a Great Lakes state. My relationship spans four generations. I buried the great-grandmother some years back. Her daughter is now in a nursing home with bone cancer and all the accompanying complications so often present. My most recent visits, along with the word I have been getting, have convinced me that she is expected to die at any time. This woman's youngest daughter is the one most visibly concerned for her welfare and also the most visibly religious in the family. At the request of this daughter and after a conversation with her, I made a decision about spiritual care.

I decided to pray with the mother and daughter through the service of the Commendation of the Dying. I consulted with the daughter, by phone, it turned out. The mother is not able to respond verbally, so we made little effort to gain her input.

As I arrived at the nursing home, another sister and her husband had arrived from out of town. I entered the room of the dying mother where the youngest daughter was waiting, too. The newly-arrived sister did not come in when she learned her youngest sister was present. Apparently she and her sister do not speak with this one. Before I began the service, I left the room and invited the new arrivals to share with us in the service. They entered, as did an aide or nurse from the staff. As I began the service, the husband and the staff person left the room. I continued the service and completed it. Then, wondering what was going on, I went to look for the two who had left. Immediately upon finding them, the husband took me to task for scaring his mother-in-law. And the staff person added her two-cents-worth by agreeing with him.

My first retort to him was that he was a death denier. I don't believe he understood what that meant. Besides being frustrated, I was in a hurry and I left without any attempt to clarify the situation. I honestly feel that no amount of time would have changed in any way their feelings about what I had done. The youngest daughter was pleased with the service. The man's wife, the other daughter involved here, seemed agreeable to what I had done.

Only a book full of details would begin to explain what was taking place here. The youngest daughter is a member of our congregation, her mother a nominal member. The rest of the family has little or no relationship to the church. Despite the negative responses, I believe that I made the correct decision to pray the Commendation of the Dying service with her.

Focus Questions

1. Theologically and pastorally, what are the appropriate considerations for using the service for the dying mentioned here?

2. Were the appropriate people included in the decision to hold the service?

3. Is there some way the pastor could have avoided the negative confrontation he encountered?

4. What are the ongoing needs for ministry in this situation?

PART II

The Consultation Case Study Method
by C. David Jones*

The Academy of Parish Clergy, Inc., was one of the first professional clergy organizations to advocate the adaptation of the Case Study Method as a tool to be utilized for the development and refining of pastoral skills. The method has been employed in seminary pastoral theology and pastoral counseling courses and was incorporated into the emerging Clinical Pastoral Education programs of both seminaries and other professional clergy organizations. The method which was followed, however, was that of a student model appropriate for classroom exercises by seminaries. The student model was review, *ex post facto*, of typical parish problems or pastoral counseling situations which were selected to demonstrate what might be adjudged exemplary or classical approaches by which clergy practitioners might deal with similar administrative or counseling problems and circumstances.

What has been unfortunate about the unwavering adherence to the study model is that in each instance the review of the case study has been after the fact. It has been a critique of someone's pastoral history, either good or bad. The presumption has been that the participants would benefit sufficiently from the case study exercise through the identifying of both positive and negative factors in the good and bad way in which each presenter/practitioner carried out the responsibilities of ministry, that future practice would be informed and enhanced through engaging the case study process. The element which has been sorely lacking in this study model approach is that it deprives the participants, in particular the presenters, of the tremendous help and advantage they might gain through a clinical model and approach.

---

*This chapter is adapted from C. David Jones' article, "The Case Study: A Clinical Approach," in *Sharing The Practice*, Vol. XV, No. 1 (Winter 1992): pp. 16-25, and is used with permission. The major adaptation I have made is using "consultation" in place of his term "clinical." I believe the former term is more professionally neutral, is thereby less tied to a medical model, and most importantly, focuses attention on the heart of this method.

The clinical model for utilizing the case study method is one which has been successfully and constructively followed by practitioners in medical, legal, psychiatric, social services, industrial engineering, and other professions for a long time. The time is overdue when we clergy should open ourselves as colleagues to the critique, counsel, advice, and collective wisdom of the group in addressing currently existing problems with the parish.

Physicians and surgeons on a hospital medical staff, for example, will pool their collective expertise in preparing for a complex surgical procedure in the operating room. They will work together in developing a composite diagnosis and in the post-operative treatment and follow-up during a patient's recovery and therapy. Each member of the medical team will bring to bear the experience, training, skills, and wisdom of his or her respective medical discipline or specialization in working on a particular patient's case. The case study is not simply a critique of what has already been done on the patient's behalf; it moves beyond the patient's past medical history (and the physician's past administrations) to examine critically the current and newly emerging information and circumstances in determining a course of action by which the practitioner(s) may seek the patient's homeostatic well-being.

In the same manner the partners of a law firm will pool their respective legal training, experience, skills, and wisdom in reviewing a client's law case and in jointly planning the best possible approach to ensure the success of any litigation or negotiations on their client's behalf. Engineers and designers will pool their expertise with colleagues in various manufacturing trades during research and development of new products.

The members of the Capital Chapter (Washington, D.C. area) of the Academy of Parish Clergy, like their counterparts in the Ohio and other Academy chapters, had followed the student model so strongly advocated by earlier Academy promoters of the case study approach. There has been, however, a growing conviction that as colleagues in ministry we could better benefit from moving from the student model to the clinical model, in other words, from dealing with past issues which we can no longer change or modify simply because they are already history, to dealing with current pastoral issues on an ongoing consultative basis. Chapter members have been invited and encouraged to present issues arising within the context of their current pastoral milieu and professional practice. The chapter members will engage in an ongoing critical analysis and evaluation of each respective case study, tracking the success/failure of the respective practitioner in his or her practice of parish ministry dealing with the issues surrounding each case. Instead of merely offering criticism and/or affirmation and support for what has already transpired, the group will pool its collective experience, training, skills, and wisdom in suggesting to the case presenter possible options and alternatives for ministering to the situations and parishioners involved in each respective case. The group will covenant with the presenter to support him or her with their prayers and counsel through the ongoing case study period until it is brought to a resolution, insofar as possible, to the presenter's satisfaction.

A chapter or colleague group, in this manner, could engage in a "participative" manner with the presenter in helping to seek and develop positive ways in which to meet the challenges and possibilities for ministry. Each member of a chapter or colleague group would in this way benefit from the expertise and wisdom of trusted colleagues. Confidentiality would of necessity be ensured by the covenant of the colleagues in the same manner in which the collective professional counsel of physicians, attorneys, and industrialists would guard with professional integrity the confidential nature of such clinical case studies. Any breach of the professional confidentiality would be a serious breach of professional ethics which would carry serious consequences to the practitioners and their colleagues; for this reason caution should be taken to safeguard confidentiality and maintain a high trust level.

The following outline for a clinical model (or consultation model, as titled in this book) is offered with the understanding that strict adherence to time allocations need not be rigidly followed except for the purpose of providing general guidelines which would permit the handling of perhaps several case studies on an ongoing basis in which different cases might not require the same exact

115

time allotments for the purposes of continued tracking in their respective development. For example, the initial presentation of a new case (study) might require the typical fifteen to twenty minutes for clarification, but in subsequent sessions an update by the presenter might require only five or ten minutes.

The same principle in the conservation of time might apply as well to the periods allocated to evaluation of the presenter's pastoral technique or particular practice related to new developments associated with the case. On the other hand, the evaluation process might take longer, depending on the particular nuances or subtleties and personal interactions, etc., emerging in the development of the case and its impact upon the presenter/practitioner's parish and his or her pastoral practice and ministry.

In addition to mere critical evaluation, *per se*, the clinical model should incorporate a serious and concerted effort to develop a group consensus which would offer possible options or alternatives for pastoral action by the presenter. Analysis and evaluation are part of the diagnosis which involves both (a) the spiritual health of the parish or of an individual parishioner and (b) the administration of pastoral care in an effort to respond to the circumstances or need out of which the case has emerged. During the analysis period attention may be focused primarily upon the recipient(s) of pastoral care; and during the evaluation period attention may be focused primarily upon the methodology/approach/ministry of the presenter or pastoral practitioner. During those periods the colleagues may seek to determine what is or is not working toward a positive resolution, and what may or may not be appropriate in pastoral care as the case progresses toward resolution. If a clear and accurate diagnosis is made by the colleague "team," then perhaps a prognosis can be predicted and a prescription for obtaining spiritual health may be developed in concert with the presenter.

This calls for an additional ingredient which is conspicuous by its absence in the earlier student model. The students in their classroom setting may engage in "Monday morning quarterbacking" by suggesting how the case might have been better handled or how they would have called the game plan. But the students may not yet have had to run the risk of actually "carrying the ball" and running through the hazards at the line of scrimmage and the hard knocks and blocking and tackling downfield as the ball carrier runs toward the goal line. It is only after one has handled the ball and faced the obstacles on the playing field that the hard realities of bumps and bruises hit home. In the church, as on the athletic field, there are perimeters to the playing field, and there are lines beyond which one may run "out of bounds." Clipping and fouls cost penalties in the church as well as on the football field. The colleague group can serve as "referees" to keep a pastoral ball carrier within acceptable scoring position and playing by the rules of the game (that's known as professional ethics). This involves the ingredient of consultation.

In the clinical model this ingredient should be added and could conceivably occupy the greatest amount of time; there needs to be a time for creative consultation. The group may decide to allocate ten, fifteen, twenty minutes or more to this important collective "brainstorming" effort, designed to explore possible options, alternative approaches, and the probable consequences or positive results which might be derived from each one. Then the group offers its recommendation to the presenter for a prioritized choice of options as well as its recommendations regarding obvious or possible pitfalls to avoid. The final choice, of course, is up to the individual pastor/practitioner as to what course of action he or she may elect to follow. The presenter/practitioner may opt to do nothing (that is also a choice), to wait and see, to "ride it out," to let time help heal, or to let a situation run its course and work itself out. Sometimes, as with surgeons, the medical or pastoral procedure may be carried out with professional precision and exacting care, but the patient or parishioner or parish may be lost. It happens! Only the practitioner can decide ultimately whether he or she has ministered responsibly in the best possible manner, and only God, who is the final and supreme judge and critic, can determine the final reward for faithfulness in the discharge of one's pastoral calling. What is hoped for and to be expected, is that the collective wisdom and mutual assistance of colleagues will result in positive resolutions and in the health and creative productivity of parishioners and their pastoral caregivers alike.

In such a clinical case study approach, the presider can serve an invaluable role in keeping the group focused during the periods for the initial presentation and clarification of the case, group analysis, evaluation, and consultation. Recommendations or "prescriptions" for pastoral care (or spiritual or administrative "surgery") should be deferred until all the factual information has been gathered and clarified and analyzed, and until an evaluation or pastoral care procedures have been evaluated, before the group engages in the collective development of recommendations for further pastoral action by the presenter. It is recommended that the presenter be permitted — encouraged — to participate in the consultation part of the case study process, so that the proposed resolutions may be a collective effort which involves the pastor who is directly involved in the case. If, for example, the group were to recommend some approach with which the presenter is unfamiliar or inept, the presenter should be at liberty to inform the group that although their suggestion might be an excellent one for a person skilled in the particular procedure under consideration, the presenter would not feel competent to carry out the requirements related to such a procedure. Therefore another solution needs to be found as an alternative. If no group consensus is reached, at least the presenter will have been given the opportunity to have benefited from the collective judgment and wisdom of colleagues. He or she would be able to proceed on a more informed basis with an awareness of various possible alternatives and probable consequences and benefits.

The time for presenter feedback, in this kind of clinical model, might not need to be as long as in the student model, particularly if the presenter is permitted to engage in the consultative period which would provide for immediate feedback. Nevertheless, the presenter should be given an opportunity (required) to give a formal feedback as a kind of "closure" during which he or she would be forced to crystallize ideas and to articulate a response as well as to declare intentions for subsequent action.

The final critique by a process observer remains an important element to the clinical model. It can serve to focus attention on the positive and negative factors involved in the group process and on the interpersonal relationships with the group. It might also help the group understand some of the dynamics at play in the emergence of the prognosis and recommendations and the readiness for acceptance (or rejection) of those recommendations by the presenter.

If the group commits itself to dealing with several cases of varying complexity, intensity, seriousness of attention, and possible consequences, the group may wish to establish outside limits or maximum which it will devote to each case. If so, group integrity would seem to require that only with the consent of each participant would exceptions be made to those time allotments for each case. If a particular case might require more time because of its complexity or urgency, the group or individual colleagues may wish to negotiate for time adjustments in exchange for reciprocal consideration on a basis of mutual fairness and equity.

Whatever the respective time allotments for each segment of a clinical model case study, each case review should encompass the following: (1) Presentation and Clarification — 5 to 20 minutes; (2) Analysis — 5 to 20 minutes; (3) Evaluation — 5 to 20 minutes; (4) Consultation (development of recommendations, strategy, and proposed procedures) — 10 to 20 minutes; (5) Presenter Feedback — 5 to 10 minutes; (6) Process Observation — 5 to 10 minutes.

The important factor is that the clinical model (or consultation model, as in the chapter title) would enable colleagues to provide mutual help to one another in addressing current pastoral issues and problems instead of merely reviewing them in retrospect after it is too late to help provide any constructive assistance toward possible solutions in the maximizing of pastoral care and ministry.

Case Studies

A. Leadership, Administration, And Finances
   Cases 35-40

B. Discipleship, Education, And Outreach
   Cases 41-45

C. Counseling And Relationships
   Cases 46-51

35. Equipping The Saints

I have always believed in the concept of "equipping the saints for ministry." I have proclaimed that all persons have been gifted by God and that they have been given spiritual gifts which they can employ in ministry within the Body of Christ.

As a pastor, it has been my goal to play a part in the development of mature Christian leaders who can make a difference in their churches and communities. I have long understood and appreciated the important job the pastor has in delegating to lay people the tasks and roles suited to them. The American Baptist congregation of my current ministry is in a Great Lakes city of 35,000 and averages about 210 at weekly worship.

The past couple years God has been speaking to me regarding how little I practice what I preach in regard to delegation and "equipping the saints." I have gone through some very frustrating times in these two years trying to keep myself on track with ministry, family, and personal priorities.

Recently I came to the realization that I am a pastor who is, in many ways, overinvolved with the ministry of the church. My ministry style has tended to be one which you might describe as "hands on" or "aggressive." I have made a commitment to rethink prayerfully my role as a pastor in an effort to develop a style of ministry which comes closer to my theology of ministry.

As I begin this journey, I immediately realize there are two major patterns which must be changed. Number one: For over eight years, the pattern in my congregation has been that "the pastor does it so we don't have to." When I begin to think about that pattern, I'm not sure what to expect from people. Will they think their pastor has become lazy? Will they think he is less effective? How might attitudes affect ministry? Number two: My personal struggle will be to curb my aggressive style in an attempt to actually allow the church to be the church.

Even though I begin knowing that I am on the right track, I find myself very unsure as to the best way to get where I am going. I want to gain from you some insight as to how to keep a balance between ministry to and ministry with people. What tasks are reserved only for the pastor and what things should the laity be doing in the Body of Christ? What suggestions do you have to help me accomplish my goal?

———

Focus Questions

1. How can a pastor determine if he/she is overinvolved in ministry, as this pastor states he/she is?

2. What should the pastor share with the congregation or its leadership about the struggle being faced?

3. If the pastor begins to change his/her behavior, what gains or losses will be experienced?

4. Consider how this pastor might involve the congregation in the transition described. For example, how might the pastor practice a new self-understanding even in the process of change?

36. Integrity In Preaching

This case concerns my preaching ministry in my Baptist congregation which has 200 at Sunday worship, in a Great Lakes city of 35,000.

For the past eight years I have developed a pattern of sermon preparation which largely consists of developing messages from outlines of sermons taken from the ministry of Dr. Charles R. Swindoll, senior pastor of First Evangelical Free Church, Fullerton, California. I have chosen sermon topics from the various series of messages which have been developed by the "Insight for Living Ministries" who reproduce Dr. Swindoll's messages through cassette tape recordings, books, and study guides. My practice has been to choose a sermon series and then, using the detailed sermon outlines, edit and adapt the message to fit my context and personality.

Recently it was brought to my attention that a former member of the congregation had stopped attending when he discovered that I was preaching from these sermon outlines. He had no objection to Dr. Swindoll; rather, he felt that it was inappropriate for me to rely on other resources for my messages.

This incident has caused me to take time to reflect and evaluate my sermon preparation practice. My preaching is well received at my congregation; in fact, my preaching is perceived as one of my best pastoral qualities. I do feel that I do adapt my messages to the point that they are my messages. They are not, however, totally original since I choose to rely so heavily on other resources.

In addition to my own reflection, I would like your feedback as to 1) the appropriateness of the sermon preparation method I am currently employing in my ministry; 2) your thoughts on the role of using other resources in aiding sermon preparation; and 3) when and how credit should be given for the use of these resources.

———

Focus Questions

1. Do you agree that the pastor has identified the critical issues here? Explain.

2. What is at stake in this situation?

3. Is the preacher's practice a betrayal of trust, as is implied by the disgruntled former member?

4. What are the legal limits to the use of others' materials? Where are the moral or ethical limits?

37. Help Or Hindrance?

Since American Baptist Church did not have a Pastoral Relations Committee (PRC) when I became their pastor several years ago, I asked them to form one. The congregation agreed to institute this new committee and members of Pulpit Committee agreed to serve as the PRC. The PRC is now over seven years old, and new members have rotated on and off the committee as stipulated in the church constitution. American Baptist is a congregation averaging 150 at worship and is located in a Great Lakes city of 25,000.

This year, for the first time since coming to American Baptist, I did not meet with the PRC to discuss salary package issues which were to be presented to the Trustee Board for inclusion in the next annual budget. Instead, I went before the Trustee Board at its budget meeting to share with them personally my request for a cost-of-living increase for myself and the other church staff members. I was not questioned by any person or group as to why I did not go before the PRC. It was not until after the budget had been proposed that one staff person and one church member wondered why the committee had not met.

Here is the reason. For the past six years, I have met with the committee trying to help them understand and take initiative for their role as PRC. This year I was feeling so overwhelmed with a busy schedule that I decided not to take the time to "coach" the PRC again on their duty to meet with me to discuss salary issues.

I am beginning to question whether it is really possible for lay people to provide the kind of support and encouragement their pastor needs. The time and energy I have put into this committee over the years has only added to my burden rather than provided relief. Even though I have always believed in the concept, I have not yet experienced its purported benefits.

In retrospect, I think my going around the PRC was a desperate attempt to get them to take some initiative on their own. I need help hearing you discuss the pros and cons of such a committee and sharing your ideas on what my options might be.

———

Focus Questions

1. What is the critical issue here for the pastor? Do you see it the same way?

2. If the PRC has been "coached" for years in its duties as indicated, but without success, what other options are available?

3. What, if anything, does the PRC, or perhaps the Church Council, need to hear from this pastor about this matter weighing heavily on him/her?

38. Let The Committee Decide?

Gregory is a 31-year-old ordained Baptist minister. He has been an American Baptist all his life and a member of my congregation of 325 worshipers, Colonial Baptist, since he was in high school. We are located in a Great Lakes city of 30,000. Out of school, Greg served on our staff as Youth Minister, and then enrolled at a Baptist seminary where he earned his Master of Divinity degree. Since then he has served two pastorates.

Greg and his family recently returned to Colonial Baptist because he is attempting to establish a small business and pursue opportunities in the area of new church development in our state. He is the son-in-law of Mrs. Horne, who serves as Colonial Baptist's Education Director.

Recently I was approached by Greg and his mother-in-law, Mrs. Horne, about the possibility of his joining the Colonial Baptist staff. Greg suggested he could help the congregation in areas such as youth and evangelism. Colonial could help him remain involved in ministry and keep his church pension and benefits status current.

I agreed to take the idea before the official Board at its next meeting. I further agreed that I would suggest that the Board appoint a committee to pursue the idea and bring its recommendation back to the Board.

At the next month's Board meeting, a committee of three was appointed — one from each major church board — along with Mrs. Horne and me serving as ex-officio members of the committee. One committee member worked as Youth Minister in Greg's last pastorate and finds himself recently back at Colonial Baptist, too.

Here is my dilemma. I am somewhat uncomfortable with Greg's taking a staff position at Colonial for several reasons. Some Colonial members were not pleased with his performance years ago when he was Youth Minister. Greg's reasons for leaving his last pastorate were negative and some rumors regarding his departure have made their way to us. The church budget is already stretched and appropriating funds for this new expenditure is not timely. I am already uncomfortable in my working relationship with Mrs. Horne, and the prospect of working with Greg intensifies that feeling within me.

I find myself between a rock and a hard place. On the one hand, if I support Greg's efforts to join the staff, I open myself to criticism by those who do not feel that he is the one for the job or that we cannot support another staff person. On the other hand, if I show negativism toward the idea, I risk alienating Mrs. Horne and Greg and those who support him.

I do feel that I made the right choice in suggesting the formation of the committee because it allows me to remain somewhat neutral while at the same time allowing "the church to be the church." I would like suggestions on how to guide the committee and congregation so that they make the best decision for the church. My experience indicates that too many people hide their true feelings until "the damage is done." I also have concern with pastoral authority. The Colonial Baptist constitution gives me almost complete power to fire a staff person or to prevent the hiring of one.

Focus Questions

1. The pastor seems to focus on seeing that "the right decision for the church" is made. Consider what would make it "right," including matters of need, mission, and long-range planning.

2. How is power being used in this case?

3. What place in a decision do this pastor's instincts have, i.e., his uncomfortable feeling with both Mrs. Horne and Greg?

4. How advisable is it for this pastor to remain neutral in this situation to let the church be the church?

39. Transitions That Pinch

I am learning what it feels like to be pinched in the transitions of our congregation. St. Thomas Lutheran, a congregation of 800 in a midwestern city of 75,000, has experienced a rapid growth spurt in the last decade. On the heels of building a new sanctuary with meeting rooms and office space, the members quickly moved forward. My Call came during the last third of the building program and I moved here eight years ago.

With high energy and a renewed sense of mission our congregation of then 400 members grew to the present 800. We shifted from a small family-style congregation to a medium-sized one which is fairly programmatic. Many families joining us in the past few years have come from larger congregations and bring with them a greater vision of congregational life.

Now there is a significant part of the congregation which had come through early transitional times but is not excited about the number of recent changes. They miss the time and place "where everyone knew your name" and they sometimes remind us of that. A few have pulled away from active participation. Overall, however, the people I serve are warm and welcoming; they have a good sense of hospitality evangelism. That does not change the fact that our transitions are pinching and even hurting. We already need, for example, new educational space for our children.

What did we do? We rolled up our sleeves and began envisioning together. Using information gathered from one-to-one member interviews, evaluations, congregational studies, and some creative forecasting, the people of St. Thomas realized how desperately we needed additional staff. I can't tell you how enthusiastic I was after that discovery!

Stewardship is a whole other story. The majority of new families who joined were of the "baby boomer/buster" age group, and I am noticing a big difference in both stewardship practice and congregational loyalty. Two members of the vision team warned us about our constant stewardship (read "budget") struggles, particularly in the summer months. In order to meet this head-on and add staff, we needed help. We contracted with a church stewardship company, and in collaboration with five other congregations, we began to address, challenge, and confront this issue.

Nine months ago, we elected to call a deaconess to our congregation. In March Deaconess Ellen, a talented and gifted person, came to serve us. This new venture is energizing but also requires time to nurture. I feel the pinch.

This staff addition, along with other costs, increased our current annual budget by a whopping 26 percent. For five months, our stewardship has been stressed. We expected some of this, but not as much. In May a council member became irate over an issue and decided to leave the congregation. In June another key family retired and moved south. In July a member lost a very important position and is looking for work. This seems normal, you might say, but all of these were giving more than ten percent of their income. These transitions have resulted in a loss of $16,000 in offerings anticipated.

Currently all our salaries are being paid, but mission gifts, outreach, bills, and other commitments are frozen. It is very difficult for our leadership to remain positive. Council meetings are tense. The staff realizes mission responsibilities are not being met and feels guilty. On top of that, expectations of people seem to grow! The toll shows as leadership people look tired and the welcoming seems to have lost some warmth. Nevertheless, many members and I, who envisioned additional staff, feel the decision was right for the ministry needs we have here.

Yesterday I found myself reading this question: "How can I come to understand and experience God's caring actions in the concrete situation where I find myself?" Part of the answer seems to be in partnerships.

Earlier in June I contacted the lead director of the stewardship company for advice on our summer struggles. He provided some wonderful insights and suggestions for communicating effectively with our members. With his advice and some council help, we came up with several options to deal with summer cash flow problems. There was an immediate response, but the deficit continues to grow.

During the last few months I have alerted our Mutual Ministry team about the stress on our leaders. This group of eight has been sensitive to our transitions and helpful to staff amidst rising expectations. They have also become listening posts for council members.

The opening Bible studies and the sermons I've been doing are asking the question: How can we as leaders help our people be thankful and respond with their resources within the life of our ministry together? After doing this with the church council, there were sparks of hope in our conversation.

This past August our staff organized a huge fiesta for Rally Day which celebrated our ministry together. It sent a message that despite our struggles, we as God's people come together to worship and celebrate. This was a huge success, a celebration of God's love and mission. There was leftover cash which helped us complete a pledge to an important ministry partner. The congregation has always done well at throwing a good party, and I noticed this style of celebration was reflective of a time when the size was smaller. The day's success was due to the huge number of partners involved in the planning and celebration.

Right now hope for me is God's gift of mutual ministry. Partners are incredibly helpful when the fears and challenges of transition pinch. Yet I must be honest and admit it is difficult to remain positive and hopeful. After eight years here, this is considered a long-term pastorate. Sometimes the times wear me down like sandpaper and some of the joy slips away. In partnership with me, can you help me see the options?

Focus Questions

1. How about a very direct question: Would money solve this pastor's and congregation's problems? Explain your response.

2. What dynamics would you look for or expect in this situation?

3. The pastor clearly is not counting on a quick fix. Examine the idea of finding hope in partnerships. What role would that mean for the pastor?

4. What other resources, including spiritual, can you recommend for this pastor and congregation facing these stresses?

40. Vacation Surprise

I have served for eleven years as the part-time pastor of this Presbyterian congregation in a midwestern town under 10,000. We are a small membership church of fewer than 75 active members with a strong sense of community involvement. As a result of an extensive mission study a year and a half ago we recognized that any appreciable growth in numbers would come from among those county residents who were in some way "different" from those who make up the membership of the rest of the county's churches. We discussed at length who these people were as part of a day-long retreat attended by all elders (ordained leaders) in our congregation. Among the groups we discussed was the growing homosexual population scattered around the county. We found no theological basis to prevent us from welcoming these people into the life of our congregation despite the fact that our denomination currently is struggling with its refusal to ordain "avowed, self-affirming, practicing homosexuals."

Within a few months of these discussions, a lesbian couple moved into the area and began attending our congregation after asking me if such participation was "safe." They were welcomed both by those who were aware of their sexual orientation and those who were not. They contributed to our worship (music and scripture reading, for example), Bible studies, and fellowship events for the past year. Then some of the high school youths asked if Marie, one half of the couple, could work with them on faith development, looking ahead to their leaving home and heading for college and work. I had a long conversation with Marie during which she voiced her need to be sure the church session, the governing body, was in support and would not "leave her hanging alone" if and when opposition arose because of her sexuality. Now it was time to test the words of welcome we had promised each other at the elders' retreat.

As I had indicated to Marie, I contacted the parents of the six youths who would be involved and, with Marie's permission, I shared her sexual preference and partnership status with each of them. All spoke highly of their assessment of the strength of her faith and were excited that she was willing to work with their children in this capacity. With that behind us, I went to the session with the youths' request, sharing again with Marie's permission her sexuality. The discussion was open and wide-ranging. As moderator I allowed and even encouraged the forays into various matters related to homosexuality apart from this specific situation, but finally brought the discussion back to the specific issue of youth leadership. The session concluded that this decision might be fraught with implications we had not yet considered. Since we were nearing the end of a long agenda, we decided to postpone a decision for two weeks to a special meeting. Meanwhile, all agreed to pray and to discuss the matter with other members.

In two weeks we convened and decided in an eight to four vote to accept Marie's offer and to stand by her in case of opposition. The session decided that I also would meet with the youths so we always had two adults involved. The four voting in the negative were consulted by the whole body about their willingness to support the action of the majority. All agreed. After communicating the session's action to Marie, I left for a week of conferences and another two weeks of vacation.

On my return I received a phone call from an elder with the words, "I need to talk with you right away." The elder had been fielding confused calls from members, mostly elderly women, who had been contacted by another elder, Donna, who had voted in the minority and who was now asking people if they could continue attending and supporting a congregation which would allow "such people" to lead our youth. I contacted Donna, discussed briefly the nature of the concern, and will be meeting with her tomorrow.

While Donna has not been very active in the worship life of the congregation, she has been very vocal on certain control issues in the past. It appears that she is wrestling with her role as a power broker in the church. The homosexuality issue seems to be secondary in her concern, but it serves as ready ammunition to make a bid to reassert her influence, which has been declining over the past few years. A neighbor of hers, a longtime member of the congregation far to "the right" of most others, has expressed the likelihood she would leave the congregation if this decision were made. Donna also is struggling with the recent death of her mother, who was her best friend and steady ally in most family squabbles, regularly supporting Donna in her role as family matriarch-in-waiting. This experience also is an opportunity to test the reality of our decision to seek numeric growth by reaching out to groups who are outside the traditional church setting.

Before leaving on vacation, I thought I had done an admirable job of leading the congregation through this experience. I was, and still am, proud of our elders as they have come to grips with both issues and feelings. Now I am wondering what else I may have glossed over in my enthusiasm. How can I effectively minister to Donna while also doing damage control, especially in my part-time role, which does not give me much time to devote to one-to-one work without pulling back on preaching and teaching responsibilities. I am wondering how best to employ the result of our lay leadership in dealing with this matter. In spite of the difficulty Donna is right now, the congregation needs her as a fully functioning part of the community.

Focus Questions

1. How is power being used by the several parties here?

2. What goals, in order of importance, would you set right now if you were this pastor, and how you would specifically attempt to achieve them?

3. What should this pastor say and do in the approaching conversation with Donna? What is at stake?

41. How Can We Intervene?

For more than a year I have been in touch with Jerry following his separation and divorce from his wife. I am his pastor, serving him and 600 other members of a Lutheran congregation in a midwestern town of 5,000. Jerry was engaged in months of group therapy after he and his wife came to recognize his abusive behavior in their relationship. To the best of my knowledge the therapy was successful but the marriage could not be saved. Jerry now is determined to share his experience with others, especially other men, and has sought special domestic abuse intervention training. In addition, he has sought understanding from a Christian perspective and is very aware of rationalizing about abuse which draws on biblical texts and the Christian tradition. It must be added that Jerry is neither college-educated nor a mental health care professional.

For months Jerry has been seeking to find ways to intervene in "the system" and specifically bring awareness and help to the male abuser. He has served on the board of a women's shelter. He has begun contacting people in the legal system. He has attempted to form a private agency to advance his concerns. He specifically asked to meet with our local ministerial association about his concerns. As a member of the group, I made arrangements for him to make a presentation.

At the ministerial meeting, Jerry shared several pages of written material: facts about abuse, current programs (really, what he wants to provide), and a couple helpful charts illustrating models of "power and control" and "equality." He shared his own experiences with us. He talked about the pervasiveness of abuse in our area. He spoke about wanting to concentrate on prevention.

Specifically with clergy in mind, he made the following proposal: "Pre-marital Couples Groups — 3 one-hour sessions, utilizing 'The Dynamics of Domestic Abuse,' a format developed by his agency. Data base intended to monitor program effectiveness for those making referrals." Jerry's intention in these sessions would be to increase awareness of what is abusive and/or controlling behavior, with the hope that the timeliness of the pre-marriage presentation might be preventative as well as motivating for some change where necessary. Jerry indicated he probably would charge $15 per session per couple. The question before our group was: How could we, as a group or individually, respond to his proposal? Would we support him? If so, how?

The root issue which is the concern of Jerry, and of the ministerial group, is abuse. Of particular interest is the fact that Jerry is ready to deal with men, who are usually the abusers. Often these persons have been regarded as hopeless cases. Jerry is ready and willing to do something about this, and he wants our response as clergy.

Focus Questions

1. In the pastor's eyes, what are the critical issues?

2. What options are available in response? How would you weight the following factors: instructor capabilities, liability, session content, cost, motivation to participate, requiring the course in pre-marriage work, relationship to pastors, supervision, current clergy pre-marriage counseling?

3. Is Jerry the right person to do this? If "yes," how do we work with him? If "no," how do we respond to him and his concerns?

4. What is at stake here for the pastor or others?

42. One More Fundraiser

I arrived at my Methodist parish of 200 members in this eastern state three years ago. The two congregations are in a large rural and suburban county. Village Church is in the small village where I live in the church-owned parsonage; Crossroads Church is at a rural crossroad five miles away. The congregations have been a circuit or parish for many years and get along rather well with each other. Their personalities, however, are different, at least theologically. Village Church has many well-educated members in the professions; Crossroads still has farmers and tradespeople. Theologically, Village Church is liberal and Crossroads is fundamental. Crossroads people accept change more slowly than do Villagers.

My ministry has been well accepted and well supported at both congregations. However, there is a difficulty. I have been struggling with the amount of time and effort the congregations have had to devote to raise the budget which has rapidly increased recently. The members are spending so much time on fundraisers that this hampers our programming ability and practice. Prior to the arrival of our new District Superintendent, the leaders had openly discussed the possibility of going to Student Parish Status within two or three years. The parish had been that some years ago but went full-time about 25 years ago. Their student parish time seems to have been good, albeit a year or two. Our new District Superintendent surprised everyone last month at our annual Charge Conference. After one of the Finance Chairpersons reiterated the student parish idea, he suggested that we consider at least one other option: applying for temporary help from the Equitable Salary Commission of the Conference. After conferring with the Chairpersons of Finance in each congregation, I decided to make application for help.

My question is: how much fundraising is too much? As a rule of thumb, what percentage of the church budget is it acceptable to raise by fundraisers? Is every situation different? A related question concerns what percentage of the budget should be subsidized by the judicatory unit?

The congregations I serve have suffered many member deaths, others have moved out of state, and our location is outside the "development envelope" of our county. We are in an agricultural, watershed-protected area, and little growth is taking place. We are receiving new members, but it is hard to find them. Village Church assimilates new members well; Crossroads Church does not. Village Church has one large fall fundraiser which nets nearly ten percent of our annual budget. Crossroads has many breakfasts and suppers which produce about one fifth of the budget.

Rising costs of pastoral ministry and physical plant operation are forcing small congregations like ours to make tough decisions about their future. Student parish status certainly is a possibility, although Crossroads Church would probably neither eagerly accept new theologies nor the ministry of a woman. Receiving an Equitable Salary supplement from the Conference would be a temporary boost, but I am concerned about how that would affect my congregations' self-esteem. It may, of course, postpone another decision. Other options may be enlarging the parish to include a third congregation or accepting a part-time or retired pastor. For myself, I would like to stay another two or three years. Our family likes it here.

Focus Questions

1. What is the critical issue here as the pastor sees it? Do you see it the same way?

2. What dynamics might be expected in this financially strained, yoked parish?

3. What is the pastor's stake in dealing with this programming and fundraising tension?

4. Staying focused on ministry in this kind of uncertain situation can be tough. What could be spiritually and professionally valuable for this pastor at this time?

43. Being A Pastor To Friends

My Presbyterian congregation of fewer than a hundred is located in a midwestern town. As pastor here for more than thirteen years, I have developed close friendships with many members of the congregation. Among these friends are June, a matriarch of the church, and Ellen, a relative newcomer of thirteen years to the community and church. June views the church as the people who own and operate the church building, while Ellen understands the church to be a community of people growing together and reaching out to others. A third friend, Gunther, has just experienced the very unexpected death of his wife to a fast-growing brain cancer. Gunther is an almost retired highway construction worker, not well educated and a "black and white" kind of thinker prone to taking immovable positions. All three are kind and compassionate Christians, pillars of the church and dear family friends.

Here is the problem. Gunther wanted to replace the sadly worn sanctuary carpeting as a memorial to his wife. By the time he came to me, colors had been selected and installation dates arranged. It was obviously a very important part of his grieving to see the job completed quickly and according to his vision. We talked about the necessary steps to get proper approval. He listened and agreed with me, but maintained that the job "will be done before Christmas or there'll be hell to pay." I tried to explain to him about several pending decisions which should be completed prior to the carpeting. He listened but was still insistent.

At the December session meeting, he presented his official request, reiterated his "before Christmas" position, and excused himself so that the session could discuss and act. During the ensuing discussion, June asserted that "we can't possibly install new carpeting by Christmas because the pews are falling apart and need refinishing." She also rejected the red color which Gunther had chosen because "people should be able to notice a change." There was considerable concern that delay in carpeting would postpone what everyone recognized to be important grief work for Gunther. Ellen further complicated the discussion with the reminder that the Worship Committee had discussed a need to rearrange the pews to

142

create a more communal seating arrangement for worship. June added to the heat of the discussion with assertions that the younger people really ought to be doing more of the work. A vigorous and heated discussion relating less to new carpeting than to the varying visions of the church swirled around the table. "What do you think we should do, Pastor?" was their very direct response when I intervened to bring us back to the question.

I told them again of my love for them, and I asked them to remember the love of all of us for the church. Then I went to the chalkboard and listed what I thought I had heard as their concerns raised by the carpet offer. We rephrased a few and added a couple I had combined when I should not have. Then we went through them one at a time asking of each if it absolutely had to be resolved before a decision to accept the carpeting offer. Most did not. The remainder we handled by being very careful to identify fully and hear each person's concern. The carpet was installed two days before Christmas and everyone was pleased with it. No one changed his or her vision of the church.

My official duty here had been to moderate the meeting. My friendships complicated that task, but they also allowed me a certain credibility. I am not certain whether I could have ministered more effectively were June, Gunther, and Ellen not such close friends. Given that our friendships and our differences in vision will likely continue, I wonder how I might effectively approach my pastoral role in future conflict situations.

Focus Questions

1. Identify the skills, abilities, and roles this pastor employed in this potentially explosive situation.

2. Discuss the place the pastor's friendships played, or seemed to, in the situation.

3. If the pastor had not been the moderator, how might that have affected the role he/she played?

4. What attention might be paid to the "vision of the church" theme which could be helpful for the future?

44. Unfinished Business

As a Baptist pastor in a Great Lakes state, I serve a congregation with a couple hundred at worship each week. We are located in a small city. I am part of a regular Colleague Support Group.

The afternoon session of the July Colleague Support Group was cancelled due to the fact that there was no presenter. Following the case presentation, the members of the group adjourned for what resulted in a long lunch eventually drifting into an informal group discussion.

During that informal session, our conversation focused on a former area pastor who recently became an Executive Minister, only to be dismissed from that position within his first year of service. At one point in our discussion, another Executive Minister's name was mentioned. An aspect of the continuing discussion had to do with how both of these individuals had conducted themselves inappropriately on occasion with some individuals of the opposite sex.

As the conversation continued, I found myself becoming a little uncomfortable about what I perceived to be innuendoes and negative comments which may have raised unfounded suspicions in the minds of group members, including within me. On my trip home following that meeting, I realized I was feeling guilty, angry, and frustrated. These feelings have remained with me, to a lesser degree, even to this day.

In an attempt to try to resolve some of my feelings, I have decided to bring some "unfinished business" before the group. The larger issue for me is: when is it appropriate to talk about others, and what is and is not "fair game" for discussion?

Not long ago a colleague shared with me that the last person he would confide in would be a fellow pastor. Pastors, he said, "tend to share too much about what they know with others, especially with other clergy." That comment has stayed with me.

Using the above situation as an example, I would like our group to struggle with the issue of integrity in our conversations. This is a quality I feel we all want in our conversations; yet, many a time

I find myself slipping into gossip or, at best, the inappropriate sharing of information. In fact, I hope that presenting this particular is itself appropriate.

Focus Questions

1. Consider whether this pastor was correct in his assessment or if he simply has an overly-sensitive conscience.

2. Even if the sharing of information does not break confidentiality, by what standard is it "inappropriate" for sharing?

3. What might be the theological and spiritual issues here, especially given the Christian faith's valuation of "the word" and the author's concern with integrity?

4. How might group members be helpful to one another in these situations?

45. Adding Staff

Hope Lutheran Church is a midwestern seventy-year-old congregation of 800 baptized members or 300 households. It is located in a town of 2,500 and served by one full-time pastor. Other support staff members are a three-quarter time secretary and a part-time youth worker. A major addition was completed several years ago and the current debt is $135,000. The current year's budget is $140,000.

Fifteen, ten, and finally seven years ago before I was called here as pastor, the addition of a seminary intern to the staff was discussed with interest by congregational leaders. Three years ago, three large stewardship group meetings identified the addition of an intern as a desired step for us.

With this background, nine months ago I initiated a survey of council members, asking them to indicate areas in which they would like to see additional pastoral time spent — if such time were available. I told them the purpose was not to add more hours to my schedule, but identify areas of needed ministry. Then four months ago, the day of our annual meeting, the same survey was given to the congregation, with 98 responses. Looking at the two surveys together, the lead areas of concern were: calling on the sick and homebound, doing evangelism or potential member calls, leading youth activities, crisis and other counseling, and visiting inactive members. At the annual meeting, there was a discussion of additional staffing, and 23 of 27 persons voting indicated they were in favor of additional staffing (intern or assistant pastor) if the funds were available. Several were undecided.

Two months ago at the March council meeting (of which half the members were new), I handed out a brief history of this discussion along with a possible proposal for seeking funds. I asked people to come prepared to discuss this at the April council meeting, at which time there was enough interest that four council members and I were directed to put together a proposal to survey the congregation on the subject. There seemed to be clear interest in adding staff, but on the other hand, I didn't sense this group was leaping to advocate it. The four (three men, one woman) designated to work on the proposal volunteered for that role.

These four persons and I met later in April, and I felt conversation was quite open and frank. There was a clear desire to move this issue before the congregation after all these years, but no one was betting on how it might go. After some discussion we decided to put together a survey of the congregation related to needs and possibilities. We also thought it was necessary to do some general preparation for the survey, so we agreed that there would be temple talks on the two Sundays prior to the survey's being mailed to every home. The one talk would be on the history of the issue, the second would be on the current needs and the survey being sent.

The purpose of the survey is to determine the support for adding an intern. Specifically, it asks whether the council should prepare a proposal for the October semi-annual meeting of the congregation. Clearly, the addition of an intern will be a challenge. Essentially it needs three "yes" votes: 1) the results of the survey, 2) an October congregational vote, and 3) the securing of adequate funding. In any event, the process is going to raise general awareness on the issue as never before.

***

Focus Questions

1. How would you describe the pastor's leadership role in this situation?

2. What could contribute to a positive outcome?

3. What non-ordinary ways might there be to secure funding?

4. What might be staffing alternatives should this one fail?

46. Whose Responsibility?

For several years, Ronald has been the "custodian" at Bethel Baptist Church, a Great Lakes state congregation of 165 worshipers in a city of 40,000. Ronald is a mildly retarded, single male in his mid-fifties. For the greater part of his custodial work, he has been supervised by his father. A couple years ago his father died, leaving him all alone in this world. He does have a sister in another state, but she shows little interest in him.

Recently, Ronald was admitted to a local hospital for "emotional problems." As a result of his three-week hospital stay, the Trustee Board hired Susan, a competent worker and member of our congregation, to take over the custodial responsibilities on a temporary basis. The arrangement worked so well that the Board decided to hire Susan as custodian and reduce Ronald's time to ten hours a week (about $50).

Following Ronald's release from the hospital, he came back to work for one week, but then admitted himself to another hospital again for emotional problems. After his one-week stay, I was asked by the social department to meet with Ronald's case worker. She suggested that he would not need to be placed in a group home but that he definitely needed direct supervision and support.

For many years it seems that members have taken some interest in Ronald, but no one ever became involved in his affairs to the degree that he now needs. Therefore, I have taken on the responsibility of working closely with him. The hardest decision I have had to make thus far is to accept his power of attorney. I now pay his bills, give him an allowance, and the like. I am currently in the process of talking to his banker, insurance agents, and lawyer in order to evaluate his financial condition. Many other issues require attention, too, such as deciding whether to sell Ronald's house, teaching him personal hygiene, and helping him to work through the death of his parents.

I am not sure what has been my motivation for taking on this responsibility. Initially, I think I became frustrated because Ronald was in need and no one else seemed available to help. The Trustee

Board did not seem to care about him and the members inquired about him but never volunteered to help out. So I felt obligated.

With this commitment to be custodian to the custodian, I have had to add rather large amounts of time and inconvenience to an already busy schedule. Now I am facing several important issues. I am torn between a) the amount of time being taken away from other pastoral responsibilities, and b) the role of the pastor in helping the "Ronalds" of our congregations and communities. Would you please consider with me my decision to become involved with Ronald and the stress it adds along with other pastoral duties?

———

Focus Questions

1. On what basis do you regard this pastor's decision to care for Ronald appropriate or not? Include theological and ethical matters, too.

2. At the time he consented to accept power of attorney, were there other options which went unseen? If so, what were they?

3. It seems this "problem" is easily defined as "the pastor's," but is it really just his? Consider the other dimensions.

4. What avenues and options are open to this pastor if he determines he cannot continue to be "custodian to the custodian"?

5. What might be learned from this situation generally about duties pastors get "trapped" into doing?

47. No Help Wanted!

The situation is a finance meeting to plan a stewardship program in the 150-family Methodist congregation I serve in a town in a Great Lakes state. The people involved are the pastor, the Finance chairperson, the Board chairperson, and a woman and a man — let's call them Fran and Marvin — who are serving as co-chairs of the stewardship campaign. They represent different congregations. Fran is middle-aged and a perfectionist, preferring to plan alone and dictate directions. Marvin is a cooperative and courteous young man.

The people gather for the meeting. The pastor distributes resource materials, welcomes everyone, and makes a few comments. The Finance chairperson reviews the budget, and the pastor outlines the dates for the campaign. The Board chairperson leaves the room to go and talk with someone.

Marvin begins, "Pastor, you mentioned that Rose (a well-known person in the judicatory) has expertise in stewardship. Would she be a good speaker for the celebration service?" "Yes," the pastor responds, "she would be an excellent choice."

Fran interjects, "I think we can make our plans without the pastor's help." Without acknowledging Fran's comment, Marvin continues to the pastor, "Could you call and invite her or should I do that?"

Fran comes back in, "I think we can manage on our own. I would be glad to call her. Do you have her number?"

"Yes, I do." The pastor proceeds to look it up and give it to her.

"We don't need you here," Fran says to her pastor. "We are quite capable of planning on our own. This isn't going to work anyhow."

"What isn't going to work?" the pastor inquires.

Fran goes on, "We cannot have a campaign if we are having joint services and we don't know whether we are or not. I don't appreciate being forced to work on a committee and having decisions made without my knowledge."

Marvin re-enters the conversation. "The decision was made by the boards of the congregations at a joint meeting to plan joint events. The celebration day will be observed in both congregations individually if we are no longer having joint services. If you disagree, you may certainly say so."

"We can't put our pledges in the same offering plate. This isn't going to work. Our people do not want a joint campaign."

"I don't know why," Marvin replies. "We can have colored cards and simply separate them. I don't see any reason why this will not go well."

Fran turns to her pastor. "We know more about our people than you do. We don't need your help. We are quite capable of planning ourselves." The pastor responds, laughing, "Oh, I know the people quite well, I think. I'm sure you know them well, too."

Marvin asks about the use of brochures and points to the one he likes. "That's fine," says the pastor. "Whatever you decide about brochures and pamphlets will be fine."

Again Fran says, "This isn't going to work. Our people are really going to be angry and won't pledge." The pastor responds, "Okay. If that is the way you feel, you may decide not to have the campaign. I have an appointment and must leave now, so I leave it with you to determine the plans."

This meeting was on Monday night. The next Sunday night I learn that a leader of the congregation is angry with me. She would not tell me the reason, except that I was running her friends out of the congregation. Much later, I learned that Fran had told her that I had fired her from her job as campaign co-chair. Fran wrote out the details of the campaign, however, and got one of her friends to speak. She herself made sharp comments from the pulpit about the behavior of people in the congregation. One Sunday when she was scheduled to make a presentation, she did not show up. She said she had knocked on the pastor's door to tell him about not coming, but that the pastor had refused to come to the door. The pastor did not hear the doorbell and actually was not aware of this until months later.

This woman on the committee, her friend the church leader, and the Board chairperson all are women in the same age category as the pastor. They have continued to cause a great deal of pain for the pastor, even making personal attacks. The pastor has learned, from others who have been supportive and from reflection and analysis, that the root issue is jealousy.

———

Focus Questions

1. From your reading of this case, do you find evidence to concur with the pastor's conclusion in the last sentence?

2. If the root issue is jealousy, what avenues are available to the pastor for dealing with it?

3. The night of the meeting described here, or in the days following, are there some constructive actions the pastor might have tried?

4. How can the pastor minimize the personal and professional damage being created here? What is at stake?

48. Marriage Friction

This couple in their mid-fifties was referred to me, a Disciples of Christ pastor, by a local psychiatrist. I serve a 200-family small town congregation in the Midwest, but this couple were not members. They were referred because of their poor communication and interpersonal friction. The precipitant behavior is the anticipation of their Army son returning home. The added stress of having another adult in their home appears to them intolerable. In addition, there is some unresolved grief over their older Army son who died of a heart attack on maneuvers rather recently. His death allowed the younger son to be discharged.

The husband is an only child who experienced a happy childhood until age ten when his father died. He socialized with schoolmates and then served in World War II. Upon his return home, he secured a four-year engineering degree on the GI bill, married, and built their own house. He is in good health and is active in a local church. His personal bearing suggests a Prussian general! He is unsmiling, caustic in his speech, and appears as self-righteous.

His wife Mary grew up as the younger of two girls. She regards her sister, who is four years older, as prettier and better than she. She loved her father and enjoyed riding on the log-wagon with him. Her mother was well-educated and taught school, yet she did not measure up to her family's and friends' expectations. Mary's mother had been dominated by fears and resentments, and Mary was determined not to be like her. Mary is an active church member with her husband. Her personality presents a need for dependent relationship, if provided in a nurturing way. If provided without this sensitivity, Mary reverts to whining, then manipulation and crying, and finally ends in depression. Her defensive behavior invites her husband's acrid, caustic joking which discounts her. This cycle then is closed with each of them feeling unloved and devalued, issuing in Mary's depression.

Their marital interaction takes place in this pattern. He makes a comment. She, fearing his biting comeback, responds with circuitous ambiguity (which sounds schizoid at times). He becomes angry, but fearing to aggravate her depression, jokes with such sarcasm that she feels further demeaned and actually becomes more depressed (melancholia *sans* medication).

Therapy consists of helping them learn non-discounting ways of communicating with each other, teaching them transactional analysis, getting a contract from him not to use "jokes" with his wife anymore, and discovering each other's values and how to share meaningfully. Furthermore, my giving them unconditional affirmation as persons helped them to elevate their self-esteem.

As a consequence of my involvement with them, Mary's medication has been reduced by two thirds and they are talking to each other reasonably well. They seem to have a fairly good marriage, which will probably mean the son can return once again to a nearly "normal" home.

Focus Questions

1. Do the treatment options pursued deal with the needs presented in an adequate manner? Explain.

2. What spiritual resources may have been brought to bear in this situation or what resources could be?

3. This appears to be short-term counseling. What supports, if any, can be drawn upon for long-term?

49. An Uncomfortable Relationship

Mrs. Blue is a fifty-year-old wife and mother of three children. She has been a member of Third Baptist Church for more than twenty years and an American Baptist all her life. Third Baptist, located in a city of 30,000 in a Great Lakes state, averages over 200 at worship. For ten years Mrs. Blue has held the position of Minister of Music. Even though she has no formal training in either music or Christian education, she has proven herself over the years as a very competent person who can get the job done.

There is no single event in this situation but rather a series of events which cause me concern. In the five years I have served Third Baptist, I have worked closely with Mrs. Blue, first in her role as Minister of Music, and now, for the past year and a half, as Minister of Christian Education and Music. During this time I have had an uncomfortable feeling in my relationship with Mrs. Blue. Despite the fact that we have had no major falling-out, there seems to be an ongoing undercurrent of suspicion when it comes to trusting one another. It is my feeling that Mrs. Blue will tell me what I want to hear about an issue or concern, only to say just the opposite in the presence of others.

I should add that I personally was not in favor of hiring Mrs. Blue for the position she holds. The congregation and Mrs. Blue, however, have been led to believe that I was totally in favor of the action. Now that she is on staff I want to make the best of the situation; yet I find myself continually frustrated with differences in musical taste, length and focus of staff meetings, and the like.

Because my relationship with Mrs. Blue is nebulous at best, I find it very difficult to get handles on how to improve or at least make the best of an uncomfortable situation. Since she tends to avoid conflict at all cost, it has been difficult to confront her with my feelings. The few times I have confronted her, I get the sense she is not honest with me in her response.

As you can tell, I have questions. What is the best way for me to relate to Mrs. Blue? How much authority should I assume in areas of concern such as music, length of staff meetings, and the like? How can I make the best of this less-than-ideal situation?

Focus Questions

1. Is the discomfort of this pastor an important issue, or should it simply be lived with? How would you determine the difference?

2. Consider whether there is a role for a third party here, such as a Personnel Committee.

3. How is the mission of the congregation relevant to this conflict as the pastor continues to deal with it?

50. Forgiven And Restored?

Ted grew up in Landmark Baptist Church, a 200-member congregation in our city of 35,000 in this Great Lakes state. At the age of 55 he has held every lay position and office possible. He has been the most prominent member of Landmark over the years. Ted is considered by most members as a "church boss," a person who calls the shots in the life of the church.

Tom, who is just a bit older, also has a long history of involvement with Landmark Baptist. His family and Ted's have been very close over the years. They socialize regularly together, take family vacations with each other, and own summer cottages next door to one another.

One day Tom came into my office and informed me that he had just discovered that his wife (more than twenty years his junior) had been having an extramarital affair with Ted for the past four years. One of the consequences of this knowledge was that Tom decided it would be impossible for his family to continue to attend Landmark Baptist Church.

It became my goal to follow the biblical prescription for church discipline as outlined in Matthew 18:15-20. My personal confrontation with Ted was futile: he told me the matter was none of my business. I shared with him that my next step would be to bring in three church leaders in order to establish fairness in dealing with this situation as well as to protect myself from any misunderstanding.

The committee wrote Ted a letter asking him to meet with us for the purpose of confessing his sin and beginning a process of restoration. Ted initially refused, but on the evening before we were to take the matter to the Board, he agreed to meet.

At the meeting, Ted confessed to the affair and stated remorse over his sin. In addition Ted announced that he would be leaving Landmark indefinitely because he was not interested in our "program" of restoration.

Not long after Ted's confession, I received information from two individuals which strongly suggested that Ted was not honest with the committee regarding his past sexual activity. It has also become apparent that Ted has a reputation for being extremely dishonest and unchristian in his business dealings.

One year has now passed since Tom walked into my office with the news of the affair. Since that time, he and his wife have joined another church. Ted and his wife have been visiting other congregations. This past Sunday, while I was away on vacation, Ted and his wife were in attendance again at Landmark.

As I look at this situation, it is truly amazing to see how God has worked through this difficult situation. The "Matthew 18 principle" has proven to be an excellent guideline to follow. Even though Ted refused to submit himself to the process, I believe the church has been served and our Lord has been honored.

Presently I am unsure as to how I should respond to Ted's return, should he stay with us. He is a divisive person who has held the congregation in bondage for years with his power. Now the church has begun to prosper significantly in his absence. On the other hand, Ted is a child of God, covered by the same unconditional love and grace in which we all share. Where is the balance between accountability and forgiveness, I wonder.

Focus Questions

1. How would you describe the critical issue here?

2. The pastor responded assertively in applying Matthew 18 to Ted's situation and saw God's hand at work in it. Using it as a guideline, do you concur with his evaluation?

3. If the goal of Matthew 18 is restoration, does it give any help to the pastor's concluding question?

51. What Mary Saw

The Russells are a hardworking middle-class family who, through good management and planning, have moved into a very attractive home in a very good community and neighborhood. They have two well-behaved and bright children who are quite involved in church school and fellowship groups. The parents, too, have been fairly active in our United Church of Christ congregation of 300 adults. We are located in a Great Lakes city of 15,000.

Recently a woman named Mary phoned me, the Russells' pastor, with a concern. Mary was not a member of this congregation, but had worked with me on community projects. Bill Russell and his family, it so happened, had been delivering some canned goods for needy families at the site of her congregation at the same time that there was a mobile blood bank operating at the site. Mary inquired of Bill if he would like to donate blood since he was already there, and hopefully, that his family wouldn't mind the delay. His response was that this was fine idea. Besides, he said, he was "overdue." And no, his family wouldn't mind.

As Bill began to fill out the Red Cross questionnaire, Mary said she happened to observe something. Several of the questions on the form are, of course, extremely personal in nature, the intention being to screen out persons who might be at risk in exposure to the HIV virus which leads to AIDS. For example, "Have you had sex with someone for money within (a certain period of time)?" According to Mary, Bill worked at the questionnaire for a few moments, but then wadded it up, tossed it in the wastebasket, and then abruptly left the building. She felt that his body language communicated some agitation — anger, embarrassment, or something she was not sure of. At any rate, as he began to complete the form, clearly something had happened within him to cause him to change his plans abruptly.

As pastor to Bill and his family, how shall I respond to this newly-acquired knowledge which has been thrust my way? I have taken advantage of opportunities to visit with them, taking a stance of alertness which might indicate some underlying problem. Doing more than this seems unjustified, even though I do have confidence

160

in the integrity and good will of Mary. I have found myself wondering whether Bill's sudden departure aroused any apprehension within his wife who had been prepared to wait for him. I also wonder if I should speak to Mary again to be assured she is observing strict confidentiality about what she saw that day.

Focus Questions

1. What does the pastor have in terms of actual knowledge in this situation, and what kind of basis is this for action?

2. What motivation(s) is/are possibly at work within Mary? Are these relevant to the pastor?

3. What does observance of confidentiality mean to the several parties in this case?

4. How assertive do you believe the pastor should be in this situation? What does the pastor stand to gain or lose?

Conclusion

For fifteen years, I have been a continuous participant in a colleague group meeting to do case studies. The membership of the group has varied, and the meeting location has changed several times, but the case study method has constantly served us well in ministry. Some of our cases are included in this book.

Some Observations

It has been fascinating to observe the great variety of subjects we have touched on over those years. This book has that same variety, as illustrated by the subjects in the index. The cases are about ministry, so people situations are at the heart of many of them, with all the problems and possibilities present in our human condition. Some subjects seemed to occur with greater frequency than others, as a look at the index reveals. Financial matters, power issues, change issues, the pastor's role, and a wide variety of personal struggles top the list. These would surprise no pastor.

The cases included in this book were relatively randomly chosen. There was no attempt made here to cover the full range of parish ministry. Consequently, there are areas such as social ministries and evangelism represented by fewer numbers of cases. In another sense, however, these same cases were not randomly selected. They arose out of the points of struggle and the fires of ministry wherever those burned the hottest at a given time. They were not matters of indifference to the case writers, but were presented with an urgency to learn and grow and return to congregational ministry with a bit more insight and effectiveness.

An Invitation

The case study method chapters in this book are clear that the written cases offered here are just the beginning of what case studies are about. The written case is presented to a group of colleagues, as few as four, but better six to twelve, who follow a deliberate and disciplined procedure to grow in ministry skills and wisdom. The benefits which these colleagues usually experience, moreover, also include mutual support and accountability.

The purpose of this conclusion is less to conclude than it is to invite other pastors into the case study process. Two methods are available in this book, and either will serve a small group of pastors well. It is important — and I would add this as a word of caution — to notice again that the two methods are distinct from each other. A group should choose one or the other and stay with it for a time.

While the descriptive and consultation case processes are outlined in the chapters by Glasse and Jones respectively, I am offering the processes in outline here as a simple and effective guide for proceeding and staying focused. For more details, the chapters should be referred to once again.

The Descriptive Case Process

A presenter provides the written case about a *past* ministry event, a presider keeps the group focused and on time, and a process observer keeps an evaluative eye on the interpersonal learning relationships. (In experienced groups where the trust level is high, we have functioned without the process observer's role.)

A. Clarification (10 minutes)

> The written case is presented and read silently by members of the group — or before the meeting is even better. Questions of additional information are addressed to the case presenter.

B. Analysis (20 minutes)

> The presenter is silent while participants discuss the case. Questions are asked. What dynamics are at work? What are the critical issues, the struggles, the feelings, the attitudes? What about the roles, the options, the uses of power, the issues beneath the

surface? What is at stake for the pastor? Who gains or loses here? What are the biblical or theological issues?

C. Evaluation (10 minutes)

The presenter (still silent) is evaluated in terms of professional competence and leadership. Are the goals accomplished? What difference does the presenter make in another life or situation? What skills are used or not used? What alternatives or options are there? What biblical and theological resources are used?

D. Presenter Feedback (10 minutes)

The presenter reacts to the group's discussion. How was it helpful, or not? What did it fail to understand? What contributed to new insights and/or alternatives for ministry?

E. Process Observer's Report (10 minutes)

This person reports on the collegiality of the group. How was the teamwork? Was there balanced participation? What was the trust level? Was there evidence of learning or growth in competence?

While the descriptive case method above focuses on a past event in ministry, the consultation case method deals with a *current* ministry event or situation. In the outline which follows, the reader should refer to the descriptive case method for the relevant questions. Perhaps more than in the previous method, participants in the consultation case method need to practice restraint so that their involvement does not become reduced to advice-giving.

The Consultation Case Method

A. Clarification (5-20 minutes)

B. Analysis (5-20 minutes)

> The participants focus on the recipients of the pastoral care.

C. Evaluation (5-20 minutes)

> The participants focus on the methodology, the approach, the ministry of the practitioner.

D. Consultation (10-20 minutes)

> The focus is on present and future ministry. The group may brainstorm to explore options, strategies and procedures are discussed, recommendations may be developed — all *with* the involvement of the presenter.

E. Presenter Feedback (5-10 minutes)

> The presenter reacts to the discussion, crystallizes ideas, and articulates intention for action.

F. Process Observation (5-10 minutes)

These two methods, while hardly the only ones in use by pastors or other professionals, have been tested in the practice of members of the Academy of Parish Clergy and others. The reader is invited to use one or both of them with the assurance that "they work." They also have the advantage of being almost immediately accessible in the practice of busy pastors who do not have an abundance of time for writing and rewriting. Most of my colleagues can sit down at a keyboard for an hour or two and have a case ready for presentation. And when they are not presenting a case, their involvement in the process also sharpens skills and reinvigorates ministry.

I conclude this invitation to become involved in case studies by whetting the appetite of the reader for another valuable book on the case study method. *Shared Wisdom** reflects the use of case studies in seminary field education and provides separate chapters on each step, albeit of a different method. While much of *Shared Wisdom*'s method is very similar to the methods presented here, Glasse and Jones would find important points to debate. One of the book's most attractive features, I would point out, is that it employs biblical images to illustrate the steps in the case process. The prophet Nathan's dealing with King David is, for example, "sneaking up on the truth"! A second excellent feature is the very deliberate use of biblical and theological questions, many included in a useful appendix.

So, how about it? Why not write up your own case, arrange to meet with a few colleagues, and work together on a "case for excellence" in your own ministry.

---

*Jeffrey H. Mahan, Barbara B. Troxell and Carol J. Allen, *Shared Wisdom: A Guide to Case Study Reflection in Ministry* (Nashville: Abingdon Press, 1993).

Appendix

List Of Clergy Case Writers

Glenn Borreson
Mauston, Wisconsin

Paul Christenson
Red Wing, Minnesota

Earl Davis
Muncie, Indiana

James Deitz
Amherst, Ohio

Marilyn Hanson
Rochester, Minnesota

Melvin Henrichs
Waukesha, Wisconsin

David King
New Lisbon, Wisconsin

Milton Mann
Luckey, Ohio

Tom Miller
Bloomfield, Nebraska

Thomas Morgan
Shawano, Wisconsin

David Nash
Summersville, West Virginia

Millie Peters
Alpha, Illinois

Mark Petersen
Sheboygan, Wisconsin

Vernon Rice
Roseville, Minnesota

Kevin Ruffcorn
Appleton, Wisconsin

Willian Sturgeon
Wyandotte, Michigan

Darryl Zoller
Hagerstown, Maryland

Index Of Key Subjects

(References are to case numbers)

www.ingramcontent.com/pod-product-compliance
Lightning Source LLC
Chambersburg PA
CBHW052046090426
42739CB00010B/2062